INSIDE

MANIC-DEPRESSION

INSIDE
MANIC-DEPRESSION

The True Story of One Victim's
Triumph Over Despair

Charlotte Clark

Foreword by Thomas A. Flanagan, M.D., F.A.P.A.

 Sunnyside Press, San Marcos, California

Inside Manic-depression: The True Story of One Victim's Triumph Over Despair. Copyright © 1993 by Charlotte Clark. First edition printed and bound in the United States of America.

Although exhaustive research was done for this book to ensure the accuracy and completeness of information in this book, the author and publisher assume no responsibility for errors, inaccuracies, omissions, or any inconsistency herein. Any slights against people or institutions are unintentional.

Library of Congress Cataloging in Publication Data

Clark, Charlotte M.
    Inside manic-depression: the true story of one victim's triumph   over despair.

    Appendices
    Bibliography, p. 163
    Includes index

Library of Congress Catalog Number 92-93876
ISBN 0-9633944-0-1

For Ralph,

Janie, Cathi, and Linda,

with love and gratitude,

and for everyone who has been

or is currently distressed by mood disorders

FOREWORD

Out of the twenty million people who experience depressive illness, approximately one-half will seek professional help. Many are unaware that they may be suffering from a biological illness caused by a chemical in the brain.

About 85 percent of those who receive treatment exhibit significant improvement, yet victims of mood disorders are too often unaware that their condition is highly treatable.

People need to know that successful treatment is available, be aware that they deserve it, and find a competent professional who will provide it.

Charlotte Clark, a bipolar patient of mine who has been free of symptoms since 1973, has written this insightful and sensitive book about the many characteristics of manic-depression. She explicitly reveals the deeply personal aspects of this complex and often misunderstood and misdiagnosed disorder. In addition, she offers a wealth of information. Her book clearly demonstrates that the role of the family is important, and spells out ways to cope with the problems of the acute phase of the illness.

At the same time, she dispels many of the myths about mood disorders. She offers practical suggestions and urges those with alarming symptoms to get professional help. Her own studious research is apparent. She offers further encouragement by mentioning the most recent medical research in biological psychiatry.

Considerable progress has been made in treatment, including the development of new medications that can replace or supplement those that have side effects or have proven to be ineffective for certain patients.

Inside Manic-depression should be invaluable to the friends and families of those suffering with a mood disorder, and to the patients themselves who will receive direction and hope when they thought there was *no* direction or hope.

Thomas A. Flanagan, M.D., F.A.P.A.
Certified, American Board of Psychiatry and Neurology
Psychiatric Centers at San Diego
Medical Director, Charter Hospital of San Diego
Associate Clinical Professor, UCSD School of Medicine

ACKNOWLEDGEMENTS

I am deeply grateful to the many people who shared their time and concern, as well as their knowledge and experience. Special thanks go to Thomas A. Flanagan, M.D., F.A.P.A., Medical Director at Charter Hospital of San Diego, who has been my psychiatric physician since 1985. He wrote the foreword to this book.

I also feel indebted to other skillful psychiatric physicians whom I saw more briefly. Like him, they helped me to lead a life free of mood swings. The insights gained from my doctors have enabled me to resolve many problems of long standing.

Kent Layton, M.A., P.A., Mood Disorder Program Director at Charter Hospital of San Diego did the medical edit of my book and generously shared his expertise. He is a clinical associate of the American Board of Medical Psychotherapists and psychological assistant to John P. Feighner, M.D., F.A.P.A. I am fortunate indeed to have their permission to use the Feighner-Layton Global Assessment Scale in Appendix D.

Creative writing teachers Judy Sala, Jeanne Patterson, and Wendy Haskett encouraged my efforts and helped me polish the book. Patterson did an early copy edit on it; Elizabeth Klungness and Linda Gross edited it more recently. Colleagues assisted and cheered me on: Kay Daut Alvarez, Maggie Wolf, Jean Steward, Marje LaBrache, Carolyn McMullen, and Ilse Newman.

Loving gratitude goes to my husband Ralph and to our daughters Jane Rasor, Cathi Clark, and Linda Clark Gross. They urged me to continue my efforts despite the painful memories stirred up when they read it. I cannot thank them enough for giving their unfaltering support, and for allowing me to share their innermost feelings about my illness.

Charlotte Clark

CONTENTS

PART I *Inside* My Mood Swings

PART II *Inside* Group Therapy

LIST OF ILLUSTRATIONS

INTRODUCTION

For many years my goal has been to reassure, inform, and offer hope to other manic-depressives and to their families and friends. This book reveals in depth my own experience with bipolar disorder, a more current term for manic-depression. I used the term manic-depression throughout most of the book because it is more commonly known.

I endured five years of extreme mood swings. As a result, I care deeply about every person who suffers from this biological illness, either as a patient, relative, or friend.

It took time to accept the fact that I had an incurable disease. It was a tremendous relief to discover that it could be controlled by a combination of medication, periodic monitoring, and psychotherapy.

The painful feelings experienced from 1967 to 1973 are imprinted indelibly on my memory. No one I knew had any of my symptoms, or even knew of anyone else who had them, so I felt utterly alone in my misery.

In many places in this book I have created dialogue. It closely follows what was actually said. In group therapy it was based on notes taken immediately after each session.

Information given was the result of my own experience, what my psychiatric physicians have told me, and research.

Dr. Thomas A. Flanagan's and my family's names were used

with their permission. The names and descriptions of all other persons mentioned have been changed to protect their privacy.

PART I

INSIDE
MY MOOD SWINGS

1
What's the MATTER With Me?

No man is free who cannot command himself.—Pythagoras

Normally, I was enthralled by the ocean view while driving along the Southern California coast near Marineland. On that particular day my thoughts raced as fast as the car. Oblivious to the ocean view, I turned onto Hawthorne Boulevard. After barreling over the hilly Palos Verdes Peninsula, I wheeled my bronze Mustang into a parking spot near my favorite department store.

After entering its doors, I felt an irresistible tug toward the Designer Room. Quality was what I wanted, and cost be damned, I thought. Yet I was drawn to a rack of dresses marked "Reduced." Habits were strong. I liked almost everything I saw in my size, and tingled with excitement. I selected far more than I could carry into the fitting room. Two eager salesladies at my elbow assisted me.

I tried on garment after garment, both thrilled with the selection and overjoyed to find so many in a size ten. Each dress was incredibly smart, as well as becoming. I decided I couldn't *live* without twelve of them. After all, every one of them was on sale, so my husband Ralph should approve. Besides, didn't I deserve them after economizing all my life?

The two exceedingly friendly clerks said things like, "That green brings out the color of your eyes, dear," or, "With your red hair, that dress was made for you."

But why were their voices so animated? And why did they go aside and whisper to each other like that? Didn't anyone else buy more than a couple of dresses at a time? Were they worried about my credit? No need to be. Ralph saw to that. And I was never extravagant. Well, maybe a teeny bit today, but why shouldn't I be?

Approval of the charges took some time, but I felt unconcerned about that, or the monthly payments. While I waited for the charges to be approved, and for my purchases to be put in boxes, I reflected on how I felt while shopping—like visiting royalty, I concluded.

My musing was interrupted when a clerk said, "We'll send your packages downstairs, Mrs. Clark. You can pick them up at the loading dock." She held out my two-page bill.

"Thank you." I stuffed it in my purse.

"It was our pleasure, Mrs. Clark," she purred. "Come see us again soon, dear."

"I will. Don't know when I've enjoyed shopping so much."

I soared out of the room like a hot air balloon.

While waiting for my boxes to be put in the trunk, I took a tissue from my purse. The bill fell out. The total was an outrageous amount, more than I usually spent on clothes in an entire year. Oh well, no problem.

During the drive home, the air leaked out of my balloon. Never had I bought so many clothes at one time. Would Ralph think I was out of my mind? How could I justify buying so *many* dresses? I decided to hide all but two in the guest room closet, and bring out the others a few at a time. Perhaps my buying spree would not be a problem after all.

But it was.

As it occurred to me that I might have been a bit carried away with my purchases, guilt's forceps first nipped me. They grabbed me a few days later, when I saw the dresses I had hidden in the guest closet. At that time, those forceps grasped me in their painful clutches.

An onslaught of depression changed everything. Though I had hidden most of the dresses, as planned, I could not think clearly enough to intercept the bill from the store.

Ralph, a meticulous manager of our income, was apparently shocked when he received the invoice that brought to light my irrational spending.

"Charlotte," he yelled from his desk in the next room.

I jumped. By then I had sunk deeper and deeper into depression. My ears were sensitive to any loud noises. Despondency immobilized me.

My feet dragged as I made my way. I stood before him, hair uncombed, no make-up, wearing a robe that probably needed washing. I saw the telltale invoice in his hand. Looking down at my fidgety toes, I shifted my weight, then wailed, "They'll put me in jail, won't they?"

"No, there's no need to worry about that."

"I'm soooo sorry. I just felt," I gulped, "compelled to buy them, and they *were* all on sale."

At thirteen I had felt the same way—my guilt feelings were excruciating. Although normally docile, one night I had defied my strict step-father after going to bed. I sneaked out my bedroom window to meet my friend Kenny at the nearest corner. We walked to the playground of a nearby grammar school.

We swung on the swings and talked and laughed about how clever we were to get away from home while our dominating parents thought we were asleep.

When I quietly re-entered my bedroom window, Mother was in my bed! Explanations had been as useless then as they were when Ralph saw the statement for my twelve dresses.

He groaned, after hearing my flimsy excuses, but said no more. I slunk away, but heard him call the store and verify his suspicion that sale merchandise was not returnable.

When he told me a few days later that he thought it best to cancel my charge plates for the time being, I went into the bedroom and threw myself onto the bed face down. I felt like crying, but couldn't shed a tear. It was as if my tears were turned off like a faucet. I did not blame Ralph, but felt terribly ashamed.

For a long time I bought no clothes.

Within two months I went from the "I can do nothing" phase to the "I can do *anything* stage, and don't tell me I can't." Both the downs and ups averaged two months. That timing evolved into a pattern for me.

If only someone—anyone—would have said, "I know exactly how you feel. I've been there, but I'm fine now." Nobody did. I felt out of step with the rest of the human race.

About three times a year my mind, body, and speech raced. I persistently did or said anything that came to mind. Confidence at times became arrogance. Anyone's opposition was futile, yet normally I sought out and respected the opinions of others.

My words could not keep up with my thoughts. I talked non-stop, often angrily. The ability to listen was completely lacking. I was disinterested in sleep, not from being on a treadmill of worry, but because I felt like a racehorse whipped to full speed by my mind.

There were not enough hours in the day to do the impossible number of things I wanted to accomplish. During those phases, I had unlimited energy to perform them. While depressed, I could scarcely put one foot in front of the other.

Blissfully unaware of causing any problems, my anger often exploded. I spat out the negative feelings that had been corked inside for years. Until then I had not dared to disagree with anyone. I was too afraid it would incite the same reaction it had with my mother and step-father.

As a child, when I displeased them, disagreed, or defended myself against their criticism, I received the "silent treatment" for two or three days at a time. It made me feel like a nothing—a big zero. It hurt. Other times I heard sarcastic renditions of what I occasionally dared to say. That manipulation continued into my adult years.

The "deep-freeze treatment," another name for the prolonged silence received periodically, left me with a sensitivity about being ignored when I have said something. Until quite recently, that insight eluded me.

When I had children of my own I realized that no parents could be anywhere near perfect, no matter how hard they tried.

Occasionally, when my unrepressed anger burst forth I was horrified to hear myself sound like a bulldozer in a petunia patch. Fortunately for the children, it was not aimed in their direction.

Anyone exposed to those outbursts was dumfounded. For example, friends Rose and Tony had Ralph and Linda, our teen-ager, over for dinner while I was hospitalized. They also entertained the three of us when I was depressed. Before that, Rose had repeatedly asked me to join her club. I politely declined. I had no interest in belonging to what I considered a high society group. What intrigued me was anything focused on emotional and spiritual growth.

When she and her husband came to our home for dinner, during one of my high periods, my anger erupted. When she again asked me to join her club, I told her, "I've never wanted to join your club, I don't want to join it now, and I never will join it, so for God's sake stop asking me." Come to think of it, Rose never did ask me to join after that. To my surprise, she and her husband are still our friends.

In Joshua Logan's book, *Josh*, he said that when he was manic he had an explosive temper and was often on the brink of battle. Me too, but sometimes I went over the brink. Ralph was the target for my repressed negative feelings. More than anyone else, he received the full impact of my fury, perhaps because he was the handiest. Simultaneously, I was afraid he would leave me, like my step-father had left Mom and me after they quarreled—about me. Even though he soon returned, those experiences left an indelible impression.

It is regrettable that we so often hurt the ones we love the most. I was unaware of it at the time, but that is exactly what I did.

2
Why *DO* They Do It?

Not one gleam pierces the gloom of my dark thoughts.
—T Southern

One night while depressed and unable to sleep, I relived the most awful period of my life. Like a replay, it repeated and repeated itself.

I remembered that the first bottomless depression had begun with the same pattern of sleep disturbance. After an average of two hours of sleep, I lay awake, trying not to disturb Ralph. Within ten days I became increasingly despondent and less able to do routine tasks. For the past year I had counseled others with their problems. It seemed unbelievable that I could no longer deal with my own, or even function.

I missed Ralph, who was 3,000 miles away at his Army Reserve Summer Camp at Ft. Lee, Virginia. Each day the feelings of frustration, worry, and helpless confusion intensified. I told the director of the counseling service where I worked, "I'm sorry, but I can't keep my appointments today. I feel a little depressed."

She called the following morning and insisted on picking me

up to take me to the office with her. Upon our arrival several counselors tried to help me. One of them ushered me into a counseling room. He handed me some paper and a pencil, saying, "Ask yourself what you're angry about and make a list." He patted my shoulder. "I have an appointment, but I'll be back as soon as my client leaves."

I stared at the blank paper. My mind wandered aimlessly. Although I kept trying to do what he suggested, I simply could not concentrate. Who's angry? I thought. I'm just so exhausted I can't think straight. Although normally gregarious, it soon became apparent that writing, as well as carrying on a conversation, had become extremely difficult.

In forty-five minutes I managed to write down one or two items. It seemed impossible to list my anger about any marital distress—or any other family problems.

When the counselor returned he looked at the paper, then said, "Take it home. You may think of something to add later."

Soon after the director had driven me home my two married daughters, Janie and Cathi, arrived. They came to see our teen-ager Linda and me in answer to her call. The girls fixed dinner. I toyed with my food, chasing it around the plate. When dinner was over, I overheard Janie call Ralph. She said, "Mom's real sick and we don't know what to do. We need your help."

That is all I heard. Cathi said, "Come on, Mom, let's all play cards."

I tried, but couldn't remember whose play it was. It happened so often that the girls joked about it. My spirits lifted for an hour or so, then sank again into an abyss.

Our older daughters stayed overnight. The three girls insisted on lying on the floor across the doorway of the master bedroom. I couldn't see why. Did they know that by then I was obsessed by thoughts about how I could do away with myself? I didn't think I had told them, but my thinking was so muddled I wasn't sure what I might have said.

The following morning I said, "I have the business card of a faith healer. I think I'd like to see him. My father's club foot was healed that way, so maybe this man could help me."

Cathi made an appointment and took me there. On the way she

asked me to tell her more about my father. She had never known him because of his early death.

"He was born in England and wore a brace on his leg." I said. "One evening he went to hear a faith healer speak. My father went up on the stage when the healer asked for volunteers.

"'Take the brace off your leg,' the healer instructed, 'you will never need to wear it again.' He removed it and from then on he never did wear that or any other brace."

"That's amazing, Mom."

"Yes, and I have a feeling this healer can help me."

We went to a house that must have been about forty years old, an ordinary wooden structure. The healer had me lie down on a table like medical doctors have. He waved a crystal pendant on a chain back and forth over my chest. I have no idea what he said or how he looked.

Why was he waving that thing around? I wondered. It spooked me. He seemed more like a witch doctor than a healer. My head and heart began to pound. I asked him to stop, which he did. I felt a mounting sense of panic. He helped me off the table and ushered me into his office. Shaking, I wrote him a check. He handed me a bottle of herbal medicine to take home with me.

Suddenly, something seemed to snap in my head like the sound of a dry twig when you step on it. I didn't understand it then. I don't understand it now. All I know is that my faith and hope had briefly penetrated the fog of depression. After that snap, the fog enveloped me once more.

I felt terrified, not knowing what had happened. The world looked hazy and sounded unreal. I stuffed the medicine bottle into my purse and hurried out of his office.

In the waiting room I said, "Cathi, I have to get out of here." My voice quavered. I scarcely recognized it.

When we reached home I felt so ashamed about my visit that I hid the herbal medication in my drawer under my hosiery. Cathi kept saying, "Oh Mom, I'm so sorry I took you there, but you wanted to go, and I wanted so much to help you." I tried to console her, but thought my efforts were of little help.

Later that day Janie drove me to the airport to pick up Ralph. He had taken the first plane home after her call. His arrival was a relief to us all.

After he took us out to dinner, Janie went home. It felt good to have my tall, good-looking hunk of a man home. He held and comforted me in his arms and I felt a flicker of hope when he said, "Don't worry, honey, I'll take care of you." He told me about changes at Ft. Lee, where we used to live.

Briefly I thought everything was getting better, but within an hour or so feelings of overwhelming gloom and hand-wringing helplessness returned.

For two weeks I had slept for an average of two hours each night, then lay awake the rest of the lonely night. I felt depleted by confusion and exhaustion. My head spun with worry, fear and anxiety. I felt extremely anxious about everything imaginable.

I asked myself: What have I done to deserve such misery? Would Janie survive her ghastly marriage? Cathi had been sounding so unhappy about her marriage. Would it get better? What would I do if Ralph left me like my step-father left mother after their big arguments about me? How could I possibly help Linda through her difficult teen years when I was such a mess?

Sunday morning Ralph made love to me. I felt a little better than I had, but completely disinterested. It was impossible to concentrate. What could have happened to me?

We lay in bed. He reassured me when I apologized, then said, "Can you tell me what you're thinking about, honey? You seem distracted."

"I'll try." I gulped. "We've been married ... how long?"

"Eighteen years."

"Right, and after all that time I still feel guilty about having had the girls in a boarding home."

"But it was in a private home that was licensed by the state. Besides, it was the only way you could handle it then."

"I know. I figured I had to do it so I could keep my mind on my job while getting my divorce." I lay on my back staring at the ceiling.

"So stop—"

"I still feel guilty too about our living together before you got your final decree and we could get married."

"But you didn't have enough money to make it on your own."

"That's for sure. Almost all my wages went for Janie and Cathi's care. Yet that didn't stop my guilt."

"Remember, your 'ex' hardly ever paid his child support."

"What could I expect? Before I left him the utility companies threatened to turn off the gas and electricity. He didn't pay the bills then either."

Ralph reached over and pulled me closer. "If you recall, he never did catch up on his payments, not even after you reported him to Failure to Provide."

"So I guess you're saying the only way I could survive was to live with you."

"Especially when Cathi got tonsillitis so bad and had to have an operation."

"It was a rougher time than usual."

I was quiet for a few moments before saying, "In spite of all that, and even though we were engaged, I still can't stop feeling guilty about living with you. I can't get it out of my mind."

"Don't see why." His hand caressed my neck.

"Maybe because I scorned the high morals I had."

"You insisted on paying half of our expenses."

"I know, but that didn't turn off the guilt."

He patted me. "I'm sorry, honey. I feel so helpless."

"I know. Me too."

I sighed. No matter how I justified my actions, in my mind I was an adulteress.

Day and night I hammered myself with guilt about every mistake I had ever made. During many of the wakeful hours at night the only thing that seemed certain was that I would never be well again. I felt dead inside, convinced there was no end to the pain and no hope for happiness—ever.

I was not anxious to die, but wanted to end the pain of living. The hopelessness I experienced convinced me that I was nothing but a burden to my family. Their anguish showed even though they tried to hide it. There was only one thing to do—for everyone's sake.

The dismal thoughts spun on .... Since I could no longer be of any help to the people I loved, I had to do it. But how could I end my life? Which method would be best?

As I dragged myself out of bed that dreary Monday morning I heaved a big sigh, something I often did when depressed. Things can't get any worse, I thought, but they did. I felt swept by a riptide into the worst day of my life.

Ralph left for work and Linda left for school before eight that morning. He had arranged for my friend Beth to spend the day with me. She was due in fifteen minutes.

I remembered that a month or so previously I had sat on a television panel for, of all things, suicide prevention. I heard someone say, "A razor blade doesn't hurt."

With a great sense of relief, I decided in a flash how to make life better for all of us. My world lacked reality as the accusing word, "Adulteress" spun around in the whirlpool of my mind and echoed in my ears. It reminded me of the dreamlike feeling I experienced every time the anesthetic began to take over before surgery.

I reached inside my bathroom drawer, found a new razor blade and unwrapped it. Bent over the wash basin, I quickly performed my own macabre surgery. It scarcely hurt at all, but my left wrist tingled with a peculiar shock. Too disoriented to have any sense of horror at what I had done, I felt more like an indifferent spectator.

I lay down on the bathroom throw rug, thinking that I mustn't stain the carpet. Surely I would die within a few minutes. Surprised and dismayed, I noted how quickly the blood congealed.

Oh God, I thought, I couldn't even do that right. My thoughts were interrupted by the doorbell. I had to answer it, didn't I? I wrapped my wrists in towels, still concerned about the off-white carpet, and trudged down the long hall and even longer corridor kitchen to the back door.

My friend Beth stood on the back porch, eyes widened and mouth agape. Her features and voice melted with concern as she said, "Oh, my dear, what have you done? Here, let me help you." As she came inside, she took me gently by the elbow, told me to elevate my hands, and guided me through the kitchen to the sink and the drawer where I told her I kept the towels.

She wrapped clean dishtowels around my wrists, then drove me to the nearest hospital where, in my turquoise robe, I lay in the emergency room for a long time. A little later Ralph and the director of the counseling service arrived, followed soon after by a police officer.

His arrival gave me something else to worry about. I must have broken the law somehow. They all tried to assure me that he simply had to make a report.

One nurse asked another while I lay waiting for the doctor, "Why *do* they do it?"

Did she think I was some sort of a nut who couldn't hear any better than I could think? Why didn't she realize I was hopelessly ill, and convinced that death was the only answer?

I continued to feel a sense of unreality about myself and my surroundings. Voices sounded far away, or was I the one who was far away? I felt so strange. At times I was watching a movie, yet I was a part of it. How confusing could it get?

A doctor finally came to stitch the gaping wounds in my wrists. He said I must be hospitalized. That sounded simple.

It was not.

Until nine that evening Ralph tried unsuccessfully to find, as directed, a psychiatrist on the staff of a psychiatric hospital. Beth insisted on remaining with us throughout that day, doing whatever she could to help us.

"Boy, I'm sure glad you're here," Ralph told her. He had to drive us all over the city. Whenever we reached a facility, he disappeared to discuss our situation, but he could not find a suitable place for me.

Through the depressive stupor of my mind I remember hearing that Cathi picked up Linda from school. That was a relief. One less thing to worry about. (I forgot many details of that day, but was filled in when able to ask.) She took her sister home with her, so Linda would not have to be alone. Cathi also tackled the sickening job of cleaning up my bathroom before going to get Linda.

I don't remember the dinner our girls prepared that night, but will never forget my bath. Janie sat facing me in the tub and instructed me to keep my hands up high so the bandages wouldn't get wet. She was the mommy and I was the child. Even now the thought of her nurturing care both turns up the corners of my mouth and puts a lump in my throat. My mother gave me the same sort of care when I was fourteen and had an exhausting bout with tuberculosis. She too had bathed me, but she knelt outside the tub.

During the next few days, the mist surrounding my mind lifted briefly, then closed in again. It could be compared to having messages recorded on my answering machine, only I listened to them when my mind became a bit more clear.

Most of the time guilt and remorse about my suicide attempt almost smothered me. I wondered, how could I possibly have thought suicide was the answer? How could I have done such a thing to my family? Too bad I couldn't be anesthetized against guilt. I tortured myself with shame and worried about whether I had committed a crime.

Meanwhile, Janie made every effort to find a hospital that would admit me. Her doctor recommended a community hospital, where I had myself committed.

After the necessary papers were signed, a nurse escorted me down endless tan halls. Along the way I heard her keys jangle, then one grated in a heavy wooden door with a little glass window in it.

The door slammed shut behind us. I was speechless. My legs felt wobbly. Why, I wondered, had they locked me up? Was I in jail? She led me into a barren, tan room with six hospital beds. There were no closets, just lockers.   I stared at the heavily grilled windows.

The room looked as dreary as I felt.

3

Therapy or Punishment?

The times are not as bad as they seem. They couldn't be.
—Jay Franklin

While I sat on the edge of my bed, a nurse with a face carved out of granite interrupted my despondent thoughts. "Charlotte, why don't you come with me to the day room?"

"I'd rather not. Please let me stay in my room," I said.

"Now, just come along, and don't make a fuss."

"*Please* don't make me go. I don't want anyone to see me. Besides, I'm so tired." My pleading was useless. Evidently hospital rules were not to be bent, let alone broken.

I reluctantly followed her into a bleak room rimmed with patients slumped in their chairs. Sitting down in an uncomfortable straight-back chair, I looked at my lap. Occasionally I glanced at the other patients. They looked inconsolable. I felt the same way. Some stared at TV, others into space or at the bare walls. I didn't realize it at the time, but their wooden faces reflected my own.

The following morning a nurse said, "Charlotte, I want you to help two other patients make coffee and list supplies for snacks."

They were young enough to be my daughters. Unable to make the most trivial decisions, I felt helpless. Luckily, the girls took over.

I wondered why they were there. They certainly had no trouble making decisions. They seemed perfectly normal as they chatted, giggling at times. In no time they inventoried the coffee, paper napkins, and other items, and wrote down what was needed. They quickly made the coffee in a pot that was completely different from the one I had at home. Their ability to figure out the secrets of that pot made me feel more befuddled than before.

A day or two later a nurse said, "Come with me, Charlotte." She led me into a room lined with cupboards and cluttered counters. "I want you to get these things ready for the sterilizer," she said, indicating a sink, a dozen or so stainless steel utensils, including urinals and bedpans, and a pile of paper bags.

"But what do I do to them?"

"Just rinse them off and put them into the bags."

Occasionally I dropped one with a clatter that made me jump. My fingers were shaky and my nerves were on edge. Indecision often paralyzed me, making the job a prolonged struggle. Was I rinsing them enough? Could I put more than one in a bag? Was I supposed to close the bags?

I was required to repeat that job many times, but not every day, thank goodness.

A diversion was created one day when I heard a voice screaming, "Help me! They're gonna get me, I can't stand it!" Male and female patients, like ants, suddenly appeared everywhere. I caught a glimpse of a woman with a blouse on, but no pants. She was running amuck down the hall.

Attendants soon caught up with her. They all disappeared through a door far down the hallway. Someone told me the patient was put in a padded room. A few days later she reappeared, looking as passive as before.

Another day a crabby looking nurse said, "Charlotte, I want you to go through the cartons in this freezer and throw out any ice cream that is spoiled. Oh yes, combine them if two partially full cartons are the same." She handed me a scoop and a trash bag.

Were they punishing me for what I did to my wrists? I asked

myself. No one else had to do these things.

There were sixteen or more cartons. I spent painful hours agonizing over the job. The crabby looking nurse came in periodically to watch me, arms folded across her chest. She often goaded me by saying, "Haven't you finished yet?" She emphasized the "yet." Didn't she know how torturous decisions were for me? Or didn't she care?

Surgery was performed on my wrists a few days later in another wing of the hospital. Because I had to elevate my arms for a day or so afterward, I felt as if I wore a sign that said, "Look at me, I did a shameful thing. I slashed my wrists."

Convalescence offered a welcome respite from my demeaning chores, but I felt more "different" than ever. I knew that several other patients had overdosed on pills. That left no scars. Why hadn't I thought of that?

When I saw the surgeon for follow-up I was grateful to find him a caring person—a real contrast to the staff, judging by my own experience on the ward. I wished I didn't have to return to that miserably uncomfortable place.

He smiled at me and said, "How are you feeling today, Charlotte?" He patted my shoulder as he left my room. That may not sound like any big deal, but it made me feel more like a human being. I had come to value warmth and kindness even more than before.

After my wrists began to heal, I heard a new command as a nurse led me into a room. "First sterilize, then make up this bed for the next patient." Again I wondered why I was singled out for those chores. Unable to express my feelings, I kept them to myself and struggled to do what I was told.

One happy day brightened my stay in that disheartening place. A nurse ushered me down the hall until we reached a closed door. My hands shook. What else had they dreamed up for me to do? To my amazement the sounds of the Happy Birthday song greeted me when she opened the door. Our daughter Janie and three of her four children were the singers. After they finished, they ran over to hug me and smother me with kisses. I loved it.

A long table was brightly decorated. The children were slicked up and wearing their Sunday best. The traditional cake had candles.

Janie served it with ice cream. The birthday song was sung again and there were presents. The only present I remember was the best one of all, the party. I cherished Janie's thoughtfulness. While doing my unpleasant chores, or when overcome by gloom, I often relived the party.

Ralph came to visit me every evening. On week-ends he came twice a day. He frequently brought our daughters. I was so manacled by depression that they did most of the talking.

As the weeks dragged by, I became aware that I had visitors far more often than most other patients. I felt lucky as I realized that many patients were neglected, or even rejected, by their families and friends.

A nurse named Gerta taunted me whenever she saw me. She said things like, "Are you still shuffling around here?" She looked at me as if I were a fly she had just found in her soup. Things she said, and the sneer on her face as she said them, made me want to hide. I cringed when I saw her come on duty, and wondered whether she had had Gestapo training.

It seemed incongruous that she was remarkably pretty. Her eyes were large, deep-set, and blue. Her classical features made her look as if she could win a beauty contest, except she wore her long, blond hair severely smoothed back into a bun. I thought it a real pity that her looks were at such odds with her personality.

"Clean the shower with this toothbrush," was the most degrading command she issued, after I'd been hospitalized for six weeks.

The patients used a communal shower. Several gathered around me. "Don't do it," they whispered. "Tell her off."

I wanted to, but could not do it. She might dream up something even worse for me to do. A woman walked by with cleaning supplies on a cart. I said, "What do you use to clean showers?" as I indicated the silly toothbrush.

Looking as if she regretted the rules, she whispered, "I'm not supposed to talk with the patients."

A few minutes later she came back and handed me a small bottle with liquid in it. It worked pretty well, but I have no idea what it was.

The following day, when Gerta ordered me to do another unpleasant job, even I was shocked as I said, "Know what you can do with your lousy job? You can stick it—and nail a board across it." And I was forbidden as a teenager to even say, "Nuts."

Within the hour I was released from the hospital, still appalled both by the words that spewed from my mouth and by the power wielded by them.

My sudden release dumfounded me. I concluded that the staff must have had orders to prod me into expressing my anger, on the premise that it would alleviate depression. I wondered whether there was a name for the treatment to which I was subjected. For me, it was more like punishment than therapy. It even agitated the other patients.

Several years later as Ralph drove by the hospital, he noticed that it had been closed. Imagine that, I thought. I hope the treatment I received has also ceased to exist. There had to be better ways to treat this disorder.

To my consternation, I had to return to the psychiatric ward in less than two months because of another severe depression. It had been gaining momentum for three weeks, but my cousin, thirteen, was coming from Michigan to see her brother graduate from naval training in San Diego. We had invited her to stay with us for two weeks so I thought, for her sake, I had to carry on.

The family made sure she had a good time, but I was unable to do my part. I tried, but decisions again ranged from difficult to impossible. She was puzzled about my behavior, but I had no idea how to explain my depression. I simply said, "I'm sorry, I know I'm not much fun, but I just don't feel like myself."

The morning she was to leave, Ralph drove her to the airport. That afternoon he took me back to the hospital. I dreaded committing myself to another stay in the lock-up ward where I had felt not only like a criminal, but one who was the butt of discrimination.

It seemed incongruous when Ralph told me months later how I had acted about committing myself. I said repeatedly, "No, I won't sign. You can't make me." The paper was clenched in my hand. I handed it back to him.

"But honey, I can't leave you alone in your condition."

He offered it to me again. Refusing to take it, I said, "Don't worry. I promise I won't do anything to myself."

"Honey, I can't take that risk. I don't want to commit you. It is better for you to commit yourself, better for your records, I assure you." He again held out the paper and his pen.

The admitting nurse backed him up. I reluctantly took the paper and pen over to her desk and signed myself in.

The best thing about my first hospitalization, besides my birthday party, was finding a special, lasting friend, Joanne. She was a patient there because she overdosed on pain pills. She had nauseating migrain headaches. Whenever she had one, the nurses were solicitous and kept checking to see whether they could help her. Even though she had made my stay more bearable, it hurt me to see the shower of attention she received. In contrast, I felt like Cinderella without the fairy godmother. It seemed a wonder I didn't have to scrub the floors on my hands and knees. How did they happen to overlook giving me that menial task?

The best thing about my second hospitalization was that it only lasted two weeks, preceded by five weeks of depression at home. There were a couple of weeks after my release when life seemed fairly normal.

During the second incarceration, I remember that two or three patients brought their problems to me. Each one said, "I can't tell my doctor this, but ...."

One was Judy, a petite young girl who was a hairdresser. She was more perky than the rest of us and generous about doing our hair. I wanted to help her when she confided her problems, but felt inadequate myself, so my efforts were useless. I was touched by her faith in me. At the same time I felt humiliated. I could no longer function well as a person, let alone as a counselor.

Something remarkable happened one time only during that— or any other depression—I cried. I hadn't done that in years. The tiny red-haired nurse who came into my room was actually nice to me. "There, there," she clucked, as she put her arms around me. I wished I had been able to cry before.

"I'm so glad you can release some of those pent-up emotions," she said, patting my shoulder.

While I sniffled she added, "Some patients cry practically all the time. It's a common reaction during a depression."

She encouraged me to tell her what brought on the tears.

"I feel like such a failure when other patients want my help with their problems," I told her.

"All you have to say is, 'I'd like to, but I'm a patient too.'"

"Really?"

"That's right. Don't worry about it any more. Tell them the nurses will be glad to help."

Then why, I puzzled, hadn't they made things easier for me? Like the others, she too had been aloof until that day.

The following day Judy and I talked to a gray-haired lady who was crying almost every time we saw her. She couldn't get over the loss of her husband, who had died two years before she went into the hospital. She kept saying over and over, "If only I had been kinder, it never would have happened."

We patted her shoulder or held her hand in hopes that somehow that would help make her feel better.

While hospitalized, I vaguely remember having talks with my doctor, whose name was Dr. Jeremy C. Jones. I heard that he was also the director of the hospital. I have no idea how often we had our little talks, what was said, or what his office looked like, except that he had an oak desk and a tilt-back chair. My overall impression was simply that the room was spartan, unimpressive, and drab, like the rest of the ward.

I do vividly remember one conversation. He asked me, "What do you want from me?" It was a few days before the end of my second hospitalization.

That day, for the first time, I saw him more clearly. He had a florid complexion, a square jaw, and thinning hair. I thought he looked about seven months pregnant.

Without hesitation I said, "I want you to stop me from ever having another deep depression."

He leaned back in his chair, one arm hooked over the back, looked at me with his intense blue eyes and said, "Well, in that case what you want is psychoanalysis."

He looked as pleased as if he were about to devour a giant hot fudge sundae.

After my release from the hospital I was in analysis with Dr. Jones for five years. Soon after it began my illness evolved into alternating periods of extreme highs and lows. Analysis brought no improvement. To add to our frustration, he gave neither Ralph nor me a diagnosis or explanation of my illness. That was to come much later—from someone else. The acute stage of mood swings was traumatic for our entire family. It seemed unjust that we were so uninformed. Surely more knowledge about the illness could have brought some measure of comfort. Instead, throughout the prolonged period of ups and downs we battled a nameless enigma.

Shortly after Judy, the hairdresser, and I were released from the hospital, she called to ask me to a meeting. She sounded excited. It turned out to be one that touted a pyramid plan that involved selling skin care products.

Ralph and the girls went with me that night to listen to the hype about the get-rich plan. Unable to listen to reason at that time, I signed up for it. I completely ignored Ralph's objections, which I later discovered were well-grounded. Some investors may have become rich from the scheme, but I could not sell those beauty products no matter how hard I tried. Neither could Cathi, who also fell for the hypnotic spiel that we heard.

I called Judy to see whether she had any suggestions to offer. She had moved away.

Within a week or so another brutal depression clobbered me.

4

Emotional Teeter-totter

Suffering is the surest means of making us true to ourselves
—Sismondi

I drove about ten miles each way twice a week for my appointments with Dr. Jones, who wanted me to see him three or four times a week. "I can't follow her case closely enough," he told Ralph, "unless I see her more often." That was impossible. Despite our insurance, the supplemental payments already strained our budget.

As I look back, I don't know how I managed to drive safely. My concentration was extremely poor when I was depressed; that averaged fifty percent of the time.

After spending about forty-five minutes to an hour in the doctor's reception room, (or should I say waiting room) Dr. Jones would ask me into his office. In cooler weather he wore turtle-neck sweaters with tweedy jackets. When warmer, he greeted me in shirt-sleeves and a tie. Much of the time I didn't know or care what he wore.

Whenever I went to his office as an outpatient, I lay on a black leather couch with my head toward the door. Sometimes I absentmindedly brushed crumbs off the couch before lying down. I don't recall much about the room except the blasted couch, his lounge chair, and a wall of books next to it.

I do remember vividly that I was expected to do the talking. He sat out of my sight behind my head and rarely said anything. When low, I could think of scarcely a thing to say. When high, I talked incessantly.

Sometimes he said, "What does that have to do with me?" Exasperated by the question, I said, "Nothing." I could not see any reason for him to ask. Perhaps it was a Freudian approach.

He usually ate his lunch during my appointments. As a child I had been told repeatedly, "Keep your mouth closed while you chew your food." His noisy crunching and slurping repulsed me, but I was unable to mention it. Coffee, potato chips, soup, crackers and celery were evidently his favorites. I think he must have inhaled the liquids. I felt like saying, "Must you make all those disgusting noises?" Unfortunately, I was a gutless wonder.

He often received phone calls during my appointments. I don't recall his having a receptionist. Why, I pondered, didn't he say, "May I return your call? I'm with a patient."

Didn't I count? I resented having those calls take up my expensive time, but couldn't make myself express my anger. In spite of the interruptions, at the end of forty-five minutes he would say, "We'll have to stop now."

I soon settled into a chaotic pattern of two months of hopeless lows that alternated with two months of hyperactive highs. I continued to lie on the coach and talk to my unresponsive audience for five years. Ralph and I knew of no alternatives—but how we wished we did.

During each one of the depressive phases I felt completely alone in my misery. Surely other individuals had been afflicted by the same symptoms. I longed to hear someone—anyone—say, "I know exactly how you feel. I've been there, but I am fine now."

Instead, no one knew what had hit me. That compounded the problem. Psychoanalysis increased my feelings of isolation.

No matter how erratic my moods became or how little I was able to sleep, Dr. Jones prescribed no medication during the years I was in his care. I often wished he would offer some relief, but was unaware at that time that many analysts did not prescribe medications. I mourned for normality as the worrisome thoughts and sleepless nights dragged on.

At a talkative session, while manic, I remember opening up about my childhood. I told the doctor, "I was an only child, often lonely, but definitely not spoiled. My mother had to work most of her life. Cousins we saw occasionally became substitutes for brothers and sisters. In spite of three stepfathers, I kept seeking a father substitute, one who could be loving, rather than a specialist in rejection. When I discovered God's unconditional love, that prolonged search ended."

I was wound up and couldn't stop. "Until then, I recall that I had envied any girl friends who lived in one place all, or even most of, their lives and had their own fathers. Between ages six to eighteen I moved fourteen times. At school and at home I was always on the outside looking in at groups where I desperately wanted acceptance."

I wondered whether Dr. Jones was still there. Silence prevailed. Why couldn't he say something to let me know I wasn't just talking to myself?

After a sigh I continued, *"The Little Red Hen* was one of my favorite books as a child. It influenced my life. Like the red hen, I believe that if no one will help me, I must do it myself. That could be one thing that kept me going when I hurt the most."

The room remained silent.

"Approval was something I have always craved. Maybe that's why I have tried so hard to excel in many areas. With practically no ego strength and a submissive nature, it's been hard to do. Sometimes I've succeeded, other times I've failed, but whatever I have done I've given it everything I've got."

One time, I visited Dr. Jones in a hospital where he was recuperating from surgery. It was during one of my manic episodes, though I did not know the terminology. I thought he looked quite fetching in his blue silk pajamas and brocade robe.

In retrospect, my illness brought about distorted thinking. That was the only time he looked the least bit attractive to me.

Whenever depressions distorted my world, I lost interest in everything enjoyable prior to that time, even making love.

The simple routine habit of making a weekly grocery list for Ralph assumed monumental proportions. I read and reread the ads for several hours each week. Doing the laundry was almost as bad. How much soap did I need? How would I ever get those stains out? Those questions tortured me. Every dismal day seemed to have more hours than usual. Unlike the "blues", the depressions recurred in cycles and were far more disabling. Sometimes I felt as if I were driving an eight-cylinder car with only four of them working. Other times it seemed to me the disease was sitting in the driver's seat; I no longer sat at the wheel.

With the exception of the one occurrence while in the hospital, I could not shed a single tear. Yet I felt consumed by sadness, confusion, and exhaustion beyond belief.

Much of the time during analysis, not just one isolated instance, I wondered whether Dr. Jones actually listened to me. One time while manic, I definitely got his attention. My smoldering anger burst into flame. I felt as if I were sneering when I said, "Why don't you go pee up a rope?"

With animation he said, "Charlotte, you have made a major breakthrough."

I had no idea why he was so impressed by my spouting out the most uncouth remark I had ever heard. Evidently it was just the sort of thing he wanted to hear from me.

During a brief normal interval, Cathi and I were sitting on the couch in our living room. She turned to me and said, "Mom, did you know that while you were sick you'd sit on this couch and not move a muscle for hours? You didn't say a word when we talked to you."

"Really? I don't remember."

"It has haunted me. We even had to take you by the hand and lead you to the bathroom when we thought you should go."

I patted her knee and said, "I'm so sorry you had to go through that horrible time."

"It was spooky."

"It must have been. When was it?"

"Just before we called Dad to say we needed him."

"Then I'm not surprised."

During those relentless depressions I thought there were no improvements, but fortunately I came out of the fog long enough to remedy the bathroom problem.

I wished at times that I could be invisible. That seemed ironic. When ignored by my parents, I had hated it. Being depressed was different. Ashamed of the way I looked and acted, I was self-conscious about having anyone see me, even our daughters. Yet I took no interest in improving my appearance.

Emotionally numb, I could not smile at TV's "Laugh In," which usually evoked my raucous laughter. I wanted to be able to push a button that would slow down the pace, so I could keep up with the dialogue.

One evening I went to the horse races at Hollywood Park with a friend, unaware that it was during a manic phase. We pooled our money and bet all we had on the Exacta in the last race. We won over $500, a lot of money those days. We whooped, screamed, hugged each other, and jumped up and down. After cashing in our tickets, we drove home. I jabbered with elation all the way.

Ralph was asleep, but I kissed him awake. "Look what I won. Isn't it exciting? I waved my winnings in front of his face, feeling as skittish as the thoroughbreds at the starting gate.

The following morning, still exuberant, I said, "Hon, you can't go to work until you take my picture."

He was in the kitchen drinking his coffee. "I know you're excited," he said without looking up, " but I gotta go to work."

I walked into the kitchen. The click of my heels got his attention. He turned his head to find me in high-heeled white sandals, the white lace pants that were part of a dressy pantsuit, and a long string of pearls. I stood in a model's stance, my body angled into its most flattering position, fanned out the money like a bridge hand, and said, "Hoo, hoo, I'm ready."

My Chanel No. 5 wafted its way in his direction. It was his favorite perfume. "You're sure not making it easy for me to leave," he said, as he raced to the hall closet to grab his camera.

He was never one to be late for work; that morning was an exception. After he came home, he told me the fellows had asked him what made him late. He said he felt his face flush when he told them, "You won't believe this, but a half-naked broad waved over two hundred dollars under my nose and insisted I take her picture, so what could I do?"

About a week later, I plunged back into the muddy waters of depression. The unrelenting mood swings added to my feelings of hopelessness. With any other health problems I'd had, improvement or recovery had soon been evident. Not so with those oppressive depressions.

Nothing brought relief, not even my mainstay of inspirational reading material. I couldn't concentrate long enough to absorb what I read. At times I thought, if only someone could "kiss it and make it better," like I did for the children's hurts when they were little.

Negative thoughts about my apparently unending condition absorbed me. I struggled to redirect them to no avail. I felt painfully guilty about my suicide attempt, which I was convinced would cause the loss of my family's love. I was afraid my illness would also prevent my ever working again.

I stewed about what my handsome husband was doing while away on business trips or military duty. Women constantly threw themselves at him. How could I hope to hold him? He would undoubtedly leave me for someone exciting, attractive—and healthy. Fear accelerated into terror from time to time. I thought I would never be productive and useful in any way. Shame became a merciless partner to the sense of failure that occurred with each depression. I was certain that I had failed to reach my primary goals of being a good wife and mother.

Another goal for most of my life was self-improvement. In junior high school I used to ask my friends what I could do to improve my personality. In my teens I studied books on the subject. Later, my aim was toward confidence and spiritual growth

When we returned home to California after Ralph's two-year tour of duty during the Korean conflict, I had enrolled at a prominent charm and modeling school. It was after we had been married three years.

One motivating factor was that ever so often he teased me by saying, "She used to be a GI's sweetheart, but now she's an officer's mess." Although I knew he didn't mean it, I was determined to never live up to that image.

Years later, despite my feelings, that is exactly what happened during every depressive phase. I looked and felt like a mess.

I had also vowed that I would never again feel like I did when I was the only woman who didn't wear a hat to the first Officer's Wives' Luncheon I had ever attended. The girls and I had joined Ralph at Ft. Lee, Virginia. He and his unit were sent there to the Quartermaster School.

I felt equally uncomfortable during the recurring depressive episodes, because I was out of sync with the rest of the world.

During one manic episode I taught at a charm and modeling studio. One of my greatest achievements came from being able to give a talk to one thousand high school girls, with only two hours' notice from my boss.

When she called I protested at first saying, "I can't possibly do it. I have a hair appointment two hours from that time and my hair's covered with goop to condition my tinted red hair. I'm a sight." "But I'm desperate. You're my only hope," the director urged. "The person who planned to give the talk came down with the flu. I have a doctor appointment myself. I feel rotten."

"Well, I'll just do the best I can, but right now I don't know how I'll manage."

After putting on a basic black dress and necklace, I wrapped a scarf around my head to cover the shower cap I had donned. I added dramatic earrings and a wide-brimmed hat, hurriedly applied my make-up, and printed out a few notes.

I had a captive audience when I opened by telling them what was under my hat.

In contrast, an average day during the recurring months of depression brought *no* feelings of success. I felt completely inadequate. For hours each morning I stood like a statue in front of my closet. Or I'd paw aimlessly through my clothes trying to decide what to wear. If I eventually made a decision I wore the same thing day after day, but not until after prolonged agonizing over the decision. When unable to make any decision, I slopped around in a housecoat.

Television mesmerized me for most of the remaining time even though I couldn't concentrate enough to remember what I had seen.

Any loud noises, including the piercing rings of the telephone, twanged in my ears—overly-sensitive during those times—and made me jump.

Reluctant to talk, I rarely reached the phone in time. When I did, I said so little the callers must have been uncomfortable too.

Meal planning was difficult because of all the decisions involved. I recall making salads of lettuce, tomatoes, onions and sliced carrots for weeks on end. Ralph barbequed more than usual and sometimes helped by saying, "How about a can of hash or chile?"

He thought we needed to get out of the house and visit friends. I'm sure he had that need, but it was painful for me. Why? Because

I felt so self-conscious. My nervousness must have been contagious. Most people were uneasy around me. They apparently had as much trouble looking me in the eye as I had looking at them.

I squirmed with discomfort when anyone took Ralph aside or into an adjacent room, where they talked in hushed tones. All I heard was "she ... she ... she ...." Didn't they realize I knew they were talking about me?

In spite of those things, I will always remember the loving kindness of my family and friends. I was aware that my illness was hard on them too and hated to cause so much pain.

During that time Mother, who lived and worked in Detroit, often wrote of her concern. Almost a year after the onset of the illness I managed to write an answer to one of her letters. I labored over it for two weeks and kept a copy for myself. This is what I wrote:

March 24, 1968

Dear Mom,

You wanted to know what's happened to me. I don't really know. I keep swinging back and forth from these awful lows to highs and don't know why, or how to stop it.

Nothing I know of threw me for a loop. I don't handle frustration well and have to learn to handle it better. Life's full of it. I've been frustrated because I've botched almost everything I've done lately and it's important to me to do things well.

Not being emotionally stabilized has really frustrated me. It's embarrassing and I feel ashamed. I spent years studying before I started to help others with their problems, but my own problems overwhelmed me. I just can't put my finger on anything and say, "That's what did it."

Nobody understands what's happened, including me. I do know I've repressed my negative emotions and tried to be nice so I'd get the approval I craved. This became too important, I think.

I know too that I have a dependency conflict. I've been too dependent on Ralph's and other peoples' opinions for years. During this ghastly illness the past year I've been more dependent than ever, the very thing I've disliked so much. It's a vicious circle.

When depressed, like now, decisions are almost impossible. That humiliates me. I want to help others, not need help myself. Difficult things should be challenges, and the impossible just take a little longer.That's been part of my beliefs for a long time, but now nothing seems to work.

It bothers me that styles have changed so much and I look all fuddy-duddy now. You know I like to look nice. And in my struggle for more independence everything went wrong. I used lousy judgment, I guess.

Anyway, my feelings about myself hit bottom, but not as far as last spring during the first hopeless depression, so I used the wrong word. I've had several slumps though, that's for sure.

I don't know what else to tell you. Guess it boils down to unnecessary worry about endless things, and it's hard to talk, and reasoning and convictions that helped me before don't help any more.

Anyway, I keep trying to carry on and do some basic things, plus some others I think might make me feel better. My conflicting thoughts, about so many things, exhaust me.

About your coming here, at fifty I don't want to be a baby who needs her mommy, and besides, can anyone else really solve my problems? I think I have to do that job. I wish I knew how. I keep telling myself this too will pass. It has to.

Love,

Charlotte

Throughout my illness Ralph kept in touch with Mother by phone and an occasional letter.

After one typically wakeful, worry-filled night I told him, "Whenever I'm awake at night and depressed I keep trying to cling like a lifeline to The Lord's Prayer, but can't keep my mind on it long enough to finish. I start over and over. It's so maddening. Makes me feel stupid—frustrated too."

He held me in his arms and I felt more secure. "That's more talking than you've done for quite a while," he said. "I think you're getting better."

He was right. For a few days I felt more like myself. Then the next high period struck. The highs were bizarre in contrast to the lows. They were fun for me, but rough on my family and friends, especially Ralph, who was more closely involved.

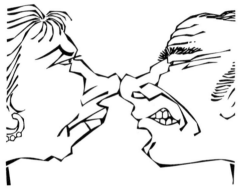

Shouting Matches

5

Ups and Downs

I became a wreck, at random driven, without one glimpse of reason, or of heaven. —Moore

Ralph and I had a series of shouting matches during a trip to Seattle. Neither of us enjoyed that trip, but we managed to get through it. We were both oblivious to the fact that our life was again complicated because I was embroiled in another high. While driving back home, the conversation was very much like this:

"We've never agreed about anything that matters to me," I said. "You've always treated the girls and me as if you were a drill instructor, instead of an officer and a gentleman." My voice became louder and louder.

"You've never carried out my discipline. You let 'em—" he said at the same decibel.

"How could I enforce punishment they didn't deserve? You're always so unfair. You never say anything nice to them. I can't stand it. They're suffering, and it shows."

"Now, just a minute. You—"

"Don't interrupt me. I'm not finished. We fight all the time. I hate fights and I hate it because I never can win."

I drew a quick breath before continuing. "I hate your drinking too and your being so damned tight and your outrageously loud snoring and snorting and carrying on so I can't sleep, and—"
"Wait a minute. Slow down. You let the girls walk all ov—"
"I certainly do not."
"And furthermore, I'm not tight, just conservative." His full lips were a narrow line as he stopped watching the highway long enough to glare at me.
"You don't scare me one little bit. I'm gonna leave as soon as we get to the next airport. I don't want to spend one more night with you."

He let me out at the Eugene, Oregon airport, where I called a friend. She urged me to fly to San Francisco to visit her.

My parting words were, "I want to be my own boss, I want a divorce, I want to be me, and nothing or nobody can stop me."

After I came home from my visit we split everything fifty-fifty and I moved into my own apartment. Our separation lasted six weeks. After dating each other, and a few others, we decided that nothing could keep us apart, including my merciless illness.

Years later I asked Ralph why he took me back. I was deeply moved when he said, "I knew you were sick. Who would take care of you if I didn't? Besides, I've always loved you, and I knew that you still loved me."

After being consumed by another depression for two months, I felt a little less gloomy. "Hon," I said to Ralph, "I've told you before, but every night after two or three hours of sleep I'm wide awake until morning. I wish we could get Dr. Jones to give me something for relief. I'm so tired and discouraged I don't know what to do."

We had just finished eating breakfast in the dining room, where we liked to eat on week-ends. The aroma of the bacon lingered in the air.

"I'm sorry," he said scowling, "I don't know what to say." He walked around the table and held out his arms. I got up, reached out to him, and felt comforted as I buried my head in his shoulder. Then my feelings of anxiety returned. We strolled into the living room. He embraced me again.

"How can I go on like this?" I looked up at him. "I've been 'way up or 'way down for almost five years now. Half the time I feel like I'm down in the bottom of a barrel."

"I know, honey," he said, looking at me as if he might melt. He gently patted my shoulder. "I guess we have no choice. We just have to weather it somehow."

Then he tightened his arms around me, which brought more reassurance than any words. I breathed a long, drawn-out sigh, something I did a lot when depressed. The stereo played our song, "Tenderly." How appropriate.

That day I saw and heard everything with clarity. It seemed strange after being in the fog of depression. I felt as if I were drifting back into the fog and told him, "My thoughts go 'round and 'round, hon, like those circles we used to draw when we had penmanship in school. Only mine are worry circles."

He leaned back and looked down at me, his eyes glistening with tears. "I wish I knew how to help you, but I don't. I guess all we can do is count on time and love to make you well."

I nodded, then raised my head, puckered for a kiss, and held him tight for a moment. We sat down and shared the newspaper. I soon put it down and looked around the large room as if seeing it for the first time. It was an attractive, tranquil looking room. I wished I could feel as attractive and tranquil as it looked.

That night, while lying wide-eyed in bed, I thought about our separation while I was "flying high." I still felt guilty about what I had said and done, but since our love had brought us together then, perhaps it could carry us through this, and any other difficult times.

Wow, I thought, I must be getting better. Otherwise, how could that hopeful thinking have crept in? Maybe we could enjoy life for a while, if I didn't zoom into another high. If only ....

For a couple of weeks I felt like myself again, capable, enthusiastic, well-groomed, and outgoing. Unrealistically, I hoped it would never end. I was able to take pride in our home, with its large Palos Verdes rock fireplace and the aqua brocade sofa with an oriental mural hung over it. Ralph enjoyed his leather chair and

I liked sitting in an off-white oriental chair or on the sofa. A large seascape hung over the long stereo cabinet. I briefly enjoyed its restful look before sailing into another high.

Whenever that happened, my mind and body became so hyperactive that I was unaware of the world around me.

I had no time to notice any roses, let alone stop to smell them. At one point I did remember Gerta, who had made life so miserable for me in the hospital. I wished her armpits would become infested with fleas, and that a horrible case of acne would erupt all over her satin-like skin. Then I wondered how I could have thought such horrible things.

During that high I whizzed into and out of my own business venture, after combatting or ignoring all of Ralph's sensible objections.

"Don't tell me I can't go in business," I said, "and I don't need to take any of those small business classes the government's offering. You've nagged and nagged me about them. I know how to run my own business." Fleetingly, I wondered whether I looked as fierce as I felt.

"I'm calling it Char's Creativity Center, and I *do* have enough capital;   I've got the $2,000 salvaged from my divorce, and furthermore, I know this is 1972, not 1930."

His efforts to reason when I was high were like trying to reform an alcoholic on a binge.   I was blissfully unaware of that.

Like a human dynamo, I was busy day and night. My mind was focused on my Creativity Center. I raced around like a car with the accelerator stuck to the floorboard. I did everything I could think of to get that business off the ground, scarcely pausing to eat or sleep. I loved every dizzy, busy minute and gloried in being the boss of three employees, no matter how inefficient they were.

Because of my tireless efforts, I managed to launch my multi-phase business venture. Char's Creativity Center had its grand opening, offered picture frames, paintings and custom framing— but not for long. I planned to add art classes and supplies, plus craft classes and supplies for them.

I had no qualifications as a business woman. What I did have was grandiose ideas and energy. I had attended painting classes for two or three years. It didn't occur to me that that did not qualify me to run a multi-facet gallery and frame shop. I *had* been told that I had a knack for selecting just the right frames for paintings. Besides, I felt omnipotent and convinced that I could do no wrong. During each high phase I also felt terribly clever and creative.

The lack of business training, experience, or more funds, were of complete indifference to me. I refused to believe that walk-by traffic was essential, and that my accountant would probably have made a better auto mechanic. I never did discover what my so-called office manager accomplished. The cute young clerk-typist I had hired turned out to be inefficient as well as inexperienced.

Ralph had suggested that I start with a small frame shop only, if I went in business at all. Instead, I felt compelled to rent a space that was about the size of a 3-bedroom home. He advised, pleaded, and cajoled, but it was impossible to break through my wall of self-righteousness.

Two brief months after my thrilling venture opened its doors, they had to be closed. I was both humiliated and broke. Months later, I admitted that I had not made one wise decision about that venture, except to go out of business.

The sledgehammer of depression hit again, I became filled with guilt and shame because I had bulldozed ahead with the business enterprise. My dreams had gone up in smoke. So had my money.

And what did Ralph do? He quietly picked up the pieces. Dozens of unsold picture frames that he stored in our garage cranked up my guilt every time I had to go in there to use the car or the extra freezer. The guilt continued to torment me throughout the depression that took over after the decease of Char's Creativity Center.

Life was such fun throughout each of the highs. During one of them, I wondered how to add a little zest to our life. Linda had moved into her own apartment, so Ralph and I had privacy in our home, though it was lonely at times.

He was going to leave for summer camp the following morning. What could I dream up to make it a special night?

I was preparing our salads for dinner. I topped them off with bits of cheddar cheese and a sprinkling of chopped green onions. Then I laughed outloud at my inspired plan. I raced into the bedroom to make some hurried preparations.

After he got home from work we enjoyed a relaxing cocktail hour. Then, gesturing toward the dining room, I said, "Sit down, hon. I'll serve dinner in a minute."

I headed toward the kitchen. The door swung closed behind me and I dashed into the half-bath nearby, after grabbing a bag I had hidden in the kitchen.

Soon after, I opened the door into the dining room, plates in hand, and glided smoothly into the room, but with an exaggerated twist of the hips. I wore high-heeled black pumps, swishy earrings, my long string of pearls, and brief black lace panties. A short black net tea apron was tied around my waist. I pivoted slowly, looking at Ralph over my shoulder. Then I leaned over him and served his salad.

The only sound he uttered was a "whee hoo" whistle through his teeth, the kind men often make at girls to show their admiration.

"Thank you," I said with a wink. Then I glided toward the kitchen, turning to do some sensuous grinds and a bump or two before disappearing through the doorway.

Dinner was a little late that night, but it didn't matter at all to either one of us.

When my emotional seesaw came down with a thump, listless days and sleepless nights again imprisoned me. I felt like a repeater sentenced to solitary confinement.

Again I neglected to do anything to improve my appearance. From morning until night I looked as if I had just gotten out of bed. Anyone who happened to see me might think I didn't know brushes or combs had been invented. After having a minimum of sleep night after night, I had no energy or animation.

My thoughts were consistently filled with paralyzing despair. It seemed increasingly apparent that the downs and ups were going to continue forever. What kind of a life was that?

Suicide was absolutely out of the question. My earlier attempt at that had done nothing but compound my problems with guilt. Not only that, the numbness in my left hand left me clumsy about handling things or typing. I dropped things so often that if I hadn't known better I might have thought I was pregnant. The ugly scars on my wrists made an announcement whenever it was necesary to turn up my hands, like for blood tests. For me, the shame has been unending, even though I knew my illness made me out of control. Worst of all was what it did to my family.

I yearned to turn off the doleful thinking as easily as turning off a water faucet, and to be stabilized emotionally. No, it didn't have to be that easy. But surely someone could bring stability back into our lives. I wished desperately that we would hear about a doctor who could help me.

Notes:

6
Turning Point

He that will not apply new remedies must expect new evils.
— Bacon

After that depression had gone on for two months, Joanne, my former hospital roommate, called. Like the fairy godmother I had lacked, she responded to my wish.

"I have a terrific new psychiatrist," she said, rather breathlessly. "His name is Dr. William Brown. He has helped me with my migraines more than all the other doctors put together. I just know he can help you too." She sounded both joyful and convincing.

"I'm so glad for you. The past five years of analysis haven't done a thing for me, or for our family, but Ralph figures we've paid for the doctor's new Mercedes. Funny you should call. I've been wishing so hard that we would hear about a doctor that could help. Maybe—"

"No maybe's. Call him. Promise you will. He was recommended by that specialist I went to see in New York. He said, 'Dr. Brown is the best psychiatrist on the west coast.'"

"That's quite a recommendation. Yours isn't bad either.

"Right."

"Besides, I can't go on forever in analysis. It isn't working for me. There has to be something that will work."

"I know there is. I spent most of my last appointment telling him about the problem you've had for so long."

"I'm overwhelmed," I stammered. "And your timing's perfect. Luckily, I must be on the way out of this depression. If I weren't, you know you would not have a receptive audience."

"I know. I checked with Ralph first."

"Well, aren't you smart?! What's your doctor's name again, and his phone number? I'll call him right away."

After hanging up, I thought about what a superspecial friend Joanne was. Imagine her going to all that trouble. Could there possibly be hope after all?

That phone call was a turning point in not only my life, but the lives of our entire family. Ralph and our girls had been loving and supportive, but bewildered and frightened too. If Dr. Brown could help me get better, it would be an about-face for all of us.

As expected, the whole family shared my excitement and hope about my changing physicians, especially since he was so highly recommended. All of us had been distressed about the treatment I had been receiving, but not one of us had any idea what to do about it, since no one we knew had the same symptoms.

Ralph and the girls had never overcome their anger at the staff of the counseling service. They did not see why they, as professionals, had not recognized the severity of my depression and the urgent need for hospitalization. The family's painful feelings had kept them from seeking referrals from that source.

With great anticipation and a tinge of apprehension, I drove downtown for my appointment with Dr. Brown. His office was in a huge medical center. It was simply furnished with a metal desk, two chairs, books, files, and an array of diplomas. I was relieved to see no couch. My feelings about his office were completely indifferent. What mattered to me was whether he could help me understand and cope with the intolerable illness that had been baffling me and my family.

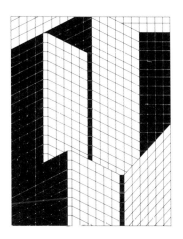

Huge Medical Center

He greeted me with outstretched hands, a crinkly smile, and a pleasant voice. His friendliness pervaded and warmed the room. I guesstimated that he was about ten years older than I. He wore a knee-length starched white coat rather than a jacket or suit coat.

During my first appointment with Dr. Brown, the first thing I told him was, "I've dreaded having to go through all that old garbage about the past."

"Charlotte," he leaned forward in his chair, "we can't do a thing about the past. Our concern is what is going on in your life right now."

"Oh my, what a relief."

In no time at all I felt at ease with this grey-haired man. His perceptive eyes conveyed wisdom and caring as well. I liked the crinkles in the corners of his mouth that showed that he smiled and laughed a lot. We faced each other while we talked. I thanked God that I didn't have to lie on a couch and do *all* the talking. Instead, he was my mentor and I was his avid student. He was also my instant friend.

"You have manic-depression," he told me, "due to a chemical imbalance in the brain. It is probably genetic." I asked him to repeat his statement, then tried to write it into my memory.

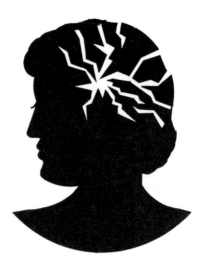

I had a chemical imbalance of the brain? My face must have shown the relief I felt about knowing that I had not caused the disorder that had engulfed me. Maybe I wouldn't have to be different from everyone else after all. Thanks to Joanne, I had acquired a doctor who presented me with the gift of hope.

Dr. Brown leaned forward again. His eyes looked into mine with obvious compassion as he said, "Charlotte, it is important that you know there is no need for concern about your illness. We have ways to treat it, so let's get to work." He exemplified serene authority.

I said, "I'll stand on my head in a corner for an hour a day if it'll help end my being an emotional yo-yo." He laughed.

"I'll do anything," I continued, "to help cure this illness. Anything."

"Not cure it, but control the mood swings."

Everything about seeing my new psychiatrist was a contrast to psychoanalysis, where I'd felt so lonely, uninformed, and even disgusted at times. Having the silent psychoanalyst sit out of my sight had often reminded me of when I had displeased my mother or step-father and they hadn't spoken to me for days. I thought that was the worst thing they could do to me. It made me feel invisible, rejected, and isolated.

Psychoanalysis had made me feel the same way.

After a few appointments with Dr. Brown, he suggested a course of treatment. "I recommend lithium carbonate, combined with psychotherapy and periodic blood monitoring. Lithium stabilizes manic-depressive illness for most people."

I hung on each word.

"After we determine the proper amount of lithium for *you*, I will only need to see you about every three months; more often for now. Any questions?"

"No, but it's great that I don't have to come two or more times a week. No offense. I would enjoy seeing you more often, but I'm glad you don't require it. Believe me, I'll do my part."

"I know you will. I don't want to see you any more often than is necessary. Here's the card of an excellent internist down your way. He will give you a physical and do some blood work. See you next week."

He walked me to the door and patted my shoulder on the way. I left, smiling to myself as I walked on rosy clouds through the long corridors and out to my car. At last life offered a promising future.

Having to be hospitalized for severe depression one more time did not change my prediction. The barrage of symptoms took over before Dr. Brown could establish the proper amount of medication for my particular needs. Patients are unique in their reactions to medication.

He highly recommended a neuropsychiatric hospital, an attractively furnished, well-managed private hospital. It looked more like a posh one-story resort hotel. A grand piano was featured in the book-lined lounge. I had the feeling of human dignity there. It made my third hospitalization much easier for both my family and me.

My five-week stay was remarkably unlike the previous hospitalizations in every way, except that both places were expensive. Ralph and I were grateful for our excellent insurance coverage.

During one of his daily visits, I said, "Honey, I can't get over how different this hospital is. No locks!"

"It sure looks different—it's homelike."

"It's lovely. So's the treatment. We get medication, but aren't zombies. We have individual and group therapy, arts and crafts, and an exercise program."

"How's the food?"

"Quite good. They even have a beauty shop. If it's okay, I'd like to have my hair done every week. I'd look better, and maybe feel better too."

He pursed his lips and gave a barely audible whistle. "Everything sounds great. About your hair, why not?"

When my doctor, recommended by Dr. Brown, asked how I felt about receiving what is commonly known as shock treatment, I simply said, "Okay, if you think it will help."

"Yes, it should shorten your depression."

"It's kind of scary, but Dr. Brown recommended you highly, so do whatever you think best."

After giving my written consent, I received ECT, more commonly known as electroshock therapy. It bore no resemblance to the version shown in "Some Flew Over the Cuckoo's Nest." My doctor, the medical director of the hospital, administered it himself, assisted by an experienced medical team.

First, I was informed about the procedure, and reassured. I was so numbed by the severity of the depression that my only thought was that if anything would help end it, I was in favor of it.

Each time it was administered, a nurse injected something in my arm. That was the last I recalled until I woke up in the recovery room.

Over the years great advances had been made in this controversial method of treatment. Faith in my doctors helped me overcome qualms about the initial treatment. Fear was no problem during the other six treatments in the series.

I blanked out parts of the current period of time, but that seemed unimportant compared to recovering from a major depression within five weeks, instead of two months or more. I did feel a little embarrassed about forgetting that some friends had taken us out to dinner when I was out of the hospital on a pass.

Ralph said, "Don't worry about it. You acted perfectly natural, even if you don't remember."

In early January, 1973, I stopped having the mood swings, characterized by extreme personality changes, and became myself again. The therapeutic lithium dosage for maximum benefit had been established according to my individual needs.

When released from the hospital, I called Joanne to tell her, "The nightmare's over, thanks to you and our wonderful doctor. I feel like a member of the human race again."

"Terrific!" she said.

"Isn't it? Funny thing, though. I don't miss the lows one bit, but I do miss the highs a little."

"You do?" Her voice was filled with wonder. "How come?"

"Guess it's 'cause that's the only time I could let my anger fly. Besides, I kind of liked feeling omnipotent."

"I've never had trouble with the anger, but I wouldn't mind some of that omnipotence."

"Know what you mean. And Joanne, I love and respect Ralph more than ever."

"Why's that?"

"Maybe partly because I think more of myself. And I love you. I'll never forget what you've done for me."

At Dr. Brown's office a week later I said, "I've found ways to stop missing the highs. I indulge myself one way or another periodically, but not compulsively."

He looked like I imagined a doting father would look.

"And I express my feelings when I'm annoyed."

"Sounds like you're doing your homework." He beamed, then looked serious. "I want you to realize that the illness you have is incurable, as I've said before, but it is highly treatable."

"Well, having an incurable illness is all right with me, as long as it responds to treatment."

It had.

The worst years of my life were over. From then on, the rosy clouds I had "walked on," after starting to see Dr. Brown, became my way of life. Once in a while I have stubbed my toe, but it was nothing more than a temporary inconvenience.

I moved ahead into a creative, emotionally stable life. During the depressions I had seen only my failures. I began to see my successes. Life became good, even if I had to depend on taking lithium or possibly some other effective medication, indefinitely. That was no roadblock for me, as long as I could remain stabilized and lead a productive life.

7

Changing Physicians

In this world of change naught which comes stays and naught which goes is lost.—Madam Swetchine

Under Dr. Brown's supervision, my mood swings became a thing of the past. Emotional stability took their place. I felt elated about the remarkable change. If I had known how to jump up in the air and click my heels, that was exactly what I would have done. In my imagination I did it.

After seeing Dr. Brown for a year and a half, something devastating brought my newly carefree life to a screeching halt. I was informed that my remarkable doctor had suddenly died.

I mourned his death as I would mourn that of a dear friend. With the magical combination of lithium treatment, and his caring psychotherapy, he had changed my life from dismal to dynamic.

For a few weeks after his death I felt as if I were on an elevator suspended between floors. I cried helplessly. How could it have happened? He was the picture of health, and the major force in my life, who had been responsible for pulling me out of my hell.

How could I find someone to take his place, someone who

could prevent my being trapped again by the mood swings?

My internist recommended two psychiatrists, but they didn't use lithium treatment. The physician Dr. Brown had recommended had moved away from our area. I felt a pang of guilt as I recalled how I acquired that recommendation.

I had felt frightened about what I'd do if anything should happen to him, such as his retiring or moving. I had no idea why I couldn't have admitted my fear and simply told him. He would have understood.

Instead, I said, "A neighbor of mine needs help, but can't drive as far as I do to get it. Could you recommend someone in our area?" He obliged.

I often wondered whether he knew why I really asked. I wouldn't be surprised. I'm probably one of the world's worst liars—inexperienced too—because it made me so uncomfortable the few times I tried it.

For a few weeks I couldn't find anyone who worked with lithium. Fortunately, I still had some capsules left. As they began to dwindle, I became a little panicky. A solution to the problem came about in an unexpected way.

Because Ralph was Army Retired, I went to the Naval Regional Medical Center at Long Beach about a cold. As I walked down the wide corridor I spotted a large banner that read "Psychiatric Services." Without hesitation I turned into the waiting room, certain that it was exactly where I needed to go.

Later, I thought that God must have known I felt desperate, so He led me by the hand.

When I shared my plight with the young man at the reception desk he said, "No problem. We have doctors who work with lithium patients."

Imagine my relief.

He handed me some forms saying, "Fill these out and bring them with you when you come in for your appointment." He made one for the following week.

The forms included the patient's medical history and many pages that revealed emotions. (See Appendix D for similar mood assessment scales.)

I spent several hours completing the forms, but my confidence increased as I finished each page. My new doctor would certainly know all about me by the time he finished looking through those papers. I felt convinced that under his care my stability would be maintained. Sure enough, it was.

Unfortunately, a few weeks later, the doctor assigned to me disclosed that he was retiring. I saw another doctor one time only, then we had to move to San Diego County so we could take care of my aging mother. With confidence, I arranged to have my lithium treatment monitored at another Naval Regional Hospital.

Two of my physicians were reassigned within about three years. Then psychiatric services became unavailable to military dependents whose husbands were not on active duty. Fortunately, I soon found a psychiatric physician who was a civilian. The lawyer who helped me manage my mother's affairs recommended him.

With the exception of the first time, changing doctors became increasingly easier. Every physician I had, with the exception of the psychoanalyst, either deepened my understanding of the illness or helped me cope with other problems.

Dr. Brown had diagnosed my illness and told me what caused it. He also helped me increase my self-confidence and improve my marriage. I was grateful for that, but most of all for ending the mood swings. I even felt thankful for having to be hospitalized again. Why? Because the psychiatric care there verified my hope that other hospitals could be completely different from the lock-up ward of the first one.

Another thing Dr. Brown did that I valued was that he saw both Ralph and me during the first few months of therapy. We worked as a three-way team. One day he cautioned, "Try to remember at all times that marriage is a partnership."

We've never forgotten his words, but sometimes we have failed to follow his advice. When that happened, we had a tug of war.

* * *

Lessons learned from other fine psychiatrists I saw after Dr. Brown's death were equally important. The first one in Long Beach helped me understand my elderly mother's behavior problems. I told him she asked for my help, but said, "No" to anything I suggested.

"How old does she act?" he asked, with a quizzical look on his face.

I pondered. "About four, I guess."

"That old?"

"Well, come to think of it, probably more like two."

"Remember that," he said, "and don't expect her to act any older. She can't. Treat her as if she were only two."

His advice often made my life easier. I've passed it on to other people when they've said, "I just don't know what to do with my mother. She's driving me nuts."

One day the same doctor said, "I wish I could give you a "guiltectomy." You are badly in need of one."

Too bad he couldn't do it. I had such unrealistic expectations of myself. (Still do at times.) They were impossible to live up to.

As a result, I have felt guilty whenever I failed to do anything right. Gradually I learned to say things like, "I goofed," or "I blew it," rather than clobber myself about it. It is far more comfortable than being defensive or guilty.

Unfortunately, that discerning doctor retired before I had made much progress in zapping out my excessive, overly strong, often inappropriate guilt feelings.

The following doctor at Long Beach, whom I only saw once, gave me at my request some printed information about lithium carbonate. It mentioned that no one should take lithium except under a physician's supervision, because it could be dangerous. It also stated that manic-depressives were predisposed to extreme moods which lithium could not cure, but could prevent.

I appreciated getting the same information from a different source, even though I had already heard it from Dr. Brown. I have found it reassuring when experts agree.

The four photocopied pages of information about lithium included cautions, side effects, symptoms of toxicity and common questions about the use of lithium.

I felt strongly that information like that should be available to all patients with manic-depression, and to their families.

Dr. Smith, Chief of the Psychiatric Unit at another Naval Hospital, was my sixth doctor in ten years. Since I had begun to research the illness that had caused me such anguish, I asked him many questions. He was an affable man who looked dashing in his immaculate white uniform.

In addition to answering my questions, he told me I could use the hospital's medical library for my research. There, among other things, I discovered that lithium had been available for two years before I terminated analysis and went to Dr. Brown.

I was furious. Both my family and I, after three years of suffering from my illness, had to endure two additional years because the analyst had not prescribed either lithium or an alternative. Later research revealed that analysts do not as a rule prescribe medication.

One day Dr. Smith suggested that I join his therapy group. He said, "It could be mutually beneficial." Those were, for me, magic words. I wanted more than anything to help others with the same illness.

The entire group proved to be manic-depressive. Like me, most of them were bipolar; one was unipolar, meaning he had recurrent depressions, but no manic episodes. They were all in the acute stage of the illness, their moods were not under control, but the intensity of their symptoms varied. I was the only one whose moods were stabilized.

Finally, I was with other people who were suffering the same way I had. I hoped to be able to tell them, one way or another, "I know exactly how you feel. I had yearned to have someone say that to me.

I also wanted to say, "I'm manic-depressive too, but I've been fine for years. You can be too." Even the thought of it excited me.

I could hardly wait to begin group therapy.

I hoped to demonstrate that manic-depressives could, with competent treatment, experience the leveling off of the mood swings. I soon discovered they could also see that when that happens it does not necessarily guarantee the end of all their problems.

PART II

INSIDE
GROUP THERAPY

8

What's Easy?

Of all mortals a critic is the silliest ... he never looks on anything but with a design of passing sentence on it.—Steele

One reason I eagerly joined Dr. Smith's therapy group was because of my admiration for him. Another reason was because he assured me that my participation would benefit the group as well as me. For a long time I had wanted to help other victims of manic-depression.

We met in a room about the size of a small living-room, but with nothing homey about it. Its vinyl floor, one drab couch, several straight-back chairs with vinyl seats, and one armchair completed the furnishings. Only one wall had windows. They were covered by Venetian blinds.

The total effect reminded me of the day room on the ward of the hospital where I went soon after the onset of my illness. An important difference was that there were no grilles on the windows, no locked doors, and no psychiatric nurses who acted more like wardens.

We were a small group, averaging only five or six people at each weekly meeting. Usually more than half were marines with ramrod backs. They wore battle fatigues tucked into spit-polished boots. The other members were predominantly young wives of marines. My gray hair made me a bit conspicuous.

After introducing me to the group, Dr. Smith said, "I would like to have each of you tell a little about yourself before we begin the discussion."

After that was accomplished, anger became the focus of attention. They could not have chosen a better topic for me. Anger was probably the one emotion I needed most to understand, express, and respond to when it was aimed at me. Even after the mood swings were under control for a decade or more, I knew my anger remained an unresolved problem.

I talked about my frustration and anger about Ralph's domination, obsessive saving of money, and shabby appearance. The group was silent for a few minutes. I figured they were absorbed in their own thoughts on the subject. A square-jawed marine broke the silence saying, "What can I do with all my anger? I'm loaded with it."

When no one else responded, I said, "Sometimes it helps me to say, 'It makes me angry when you say or do that.' Instead of accusing him I share the blame. Once in a while I say, 'I don't have to listen to that,' and leave the room."

No one said a word, but I could see the rapt attention on their faces as I continued with my pet way to handle anger. "Keep some lollipops or bubble gum handy. Unwrap one and pop it into your mouth, then hand one to your sparring-partner, saying, 'Long as we're acting like kids, we might as well enjoy ourselves.'"

They laughed. That was what happened whenever I have remembered to use that suggestion during a fight. Why didn't I do it more often? I asked myself.

When we all quieted down, Dr. Smith said, "When there is overreaction or misplaced anger you might ask, 'What are you *really* angry about?'"

A woman named Dorothy told us she worked in a convalescent home. She loved working with the patients there. Her long, brassy-colored hair looked as if she had just gotten out of bed. She had poured her bulging body into tight jeans, topped off with a huge, faded sweatshirt. Thongs completed her outfit.

The room became as hushed as a theater when the curtains first open as she proclaimed, through clenched teeth, "All men are liars and cheaters." She spat each word.

After that she ranted at length about what a louse her husband was. Whenever she took a breath Dr. Smith asked, "How did that make you feel, Dorothy?"

She ignored his question and continued to blame her husband for everything wrong with their miserable marriage, seemingly unaware that she contributed in any way to their problems.

Why, I wondered, do so many people think there are no choices available? And why do they think that others are to blame for their misery?

Suddenly, I realized that if I were asked those questions, I should plead guilty.

"Generalizations make me angry," I said. "For instance, 'I don't like to be included in 'all women.' I'm a unique individual and want to be considered one."

Dr. Smith said quietly, "Generalizations are another way to hide angry feelings. And now, it is time to close."

How could the session be over so soon? I was sorry to see it end.

As we left the building I said to Dorothy, who had among other things, told us her husband had beaten and raped her repeatedly, "May I tell you something that helped me value myself more? May sound silly, but it worked."

"Yeah, go ahead." She shifted the weight of her body, about twice the size of mine, to the other foot and crossed her arms across her ample chest. That was a defensive posture, I knew from my counseling work, but I continued.

"Stand in front of a mirror every day, hug yourself and say, 'I'm a wonderful person. I love me.' Our minister told us, 'Do it as often as necessary, and remember if you don't value yourself, why should anyone else value you?'"

"What's to like about me?"

"I think you're a loving, caring person. If you were not, how could you take care of those poor old souls you told us you work with?"

The following week, only Dorothy and a young woman named Betsey were there. Betsey's light brown hair almost hid her eyes, which had a faraway look much of the time, as if her mind were elsewhere. I felt concern and empathy for her.

Dorothy, unfortunately, disgusted me or made me angry. She constantly complained about her soap opera life, but was apparently not one bit interested in changing it. She chose to disregard anything anyone said, including Dr. Smith.

He asked me how it made me feel when Dorothy ignored what I said to her. "Angry and rejected. I've had too much of that in my life."

After the session ended, Dorothy told me, "You piss me off. You think you have all the answers."

Strangely enough, it didn't bother me. I was able to say, "I'm sorry you feel that way." I knew then that I was making progress. It made me feel good about myself.

To my surprise, she asked me to join her and Betsy for lunch. I was glad I could decline, because of a date with our daughter Cathi.

Dorothy exhausted me with her constant bellyaching. I knew I griped too at times, but I also kept trying to improve myself and my life.

* * *

While waiting for the other members to arrive at our next meeting, I thought about what a made-to-order experience group was for me. We were urged to show our feelings, and Dorothy brought out my worst ones. That provided tailor-made therapy for me.

Red, a tall, lean marine with freckles, and hair the color implied by his name, was with us for the first time since I had joined the group. He was given a rousing welcome after, I presumed, a prolonged absence.

After while, he announced, "Besides coming here, I go to a minister for counseling every week."

"Me too," Betsey chimed in.

"Good for you," I said. "I think it goes hand in hand with medication and psychotherapy. Spiritual growth has always been important to me too, but I sure got away from pursuing it during the mood swings, when I needed it most."

I reflected on the classes I had taken at our church. They focused on affirmative ways to pray and ways to cope with everyday problems. My studies had helped build my ego-strength too, but when attacked, it teetered again. I began each day with reading Unity's *Daily Word*, followed by a form of meditation learned in a church class.

My thoughts were interrupted when I heard Red say, "I've had trouble with anger most of my life." He looked down and clutched his long fingers together. "Now it's tested a lot, but I've started to get a handle on it."

"How?" someone asked.

"Sometimes I walk to cool off. Other times I just don't express my feelings 'til I've simmered down."

Betsey said, "I think I've been acting like a witch with my child." She bit her lower lip. "He's nine and a half."

A few of us told her about our own angry outbursts, especially when we were caught up in a manic episode.

Dr. Gottlieb had just joined our group as Dr. Smith's associate. He was a short, serious-looking man with black hair and a clipped moustache. He said, "Charlotte, you haven't said much about yourself, but you have offered quite a lot of advice."

He didn't endear himself to me when he said that. I felt my jaw tighten as I recalled that he wasn't with us when I spilled out a lot of my angry feelings.

I brought him up to date. "I have trouble expressing anger. I haven't had any good role models for using it. My folks wouldn't speak to me for days if I displeased them. My stepfather left us after arguments with my mom—about me. And currently my husband's unexpected push-button outbursts startle and upset me."

Once I started to respond I couldn't stop. I noticed that my hands were clenched into tight little fists.

A little later I told about our ghastly Christmas Day, ruined by our granddaughter, twenty-two. She and her boyfriend ate and drank so much that she ruined the day for everyone. Another holiday dinner at our home a few days later was even worse. One relative's rejection and snide remarks caused one of our daughters and her family to leave before dinner. I was so upset retelling these incidents that I could scarcely get the words out.

Dr. Smith said, "It is important that you communicate your feelings about both incidents. You may still be responding to childhood conditioning about anger."

"Could be. Sometimes I still feel as if I can't do anything right. In spite of all efforts I can't seem to get a handle on criticism, and dammit, I evidently still crave approval."

Eyes lowered, I stared at the floor, feeling miserable.

In a private session with Dr. Smith he said, "Charlotte, you have to cut the ties to the past and learn to express your anger and hurt feelings."

"You're right, but I'm furious with myself. I thought that after all the classes I've taken I should be able to cope with anything life presented."

He scowled as he asked, "Must you expect that much of yourself all the time?"

I hesitated. "Well, maybe it is a bit unreasonable."

We talked about my marital problems, more prevalent since Ralph's retirement.

Dr. Smith said, "It sounds like a power struggle."

After thinking for a moment, I said with awe, "I think you've nailed it. I rebel at his having so much control over me and over our life. What *I* want is a partnership."

"Four events cause people the most trouble, Charlotte: loss of a loved one, divorce, moving, and retirement."

"Good grief! Ralph retired less than a year ago, shortly before our recent move down here. Maybe we still haven't adjusted to that double whammy."

"What has gone on since his retirement?"

"He has no engrossing hobbies or interests, except an occasional short game of golf. He finds it necessary to tell me how to do everything I've been doing for the past thirty years or more. I've had it up to here," I put the palm of my hand over my head, " when it comes to togetherness. I feel as if my territory has been taken over. Lots of times I realize I love him, but I don't like him very much."

"Do you know why?"

"Because I feel dominated and criticised too much and I have lost my freedom. We had no conditioning for retirement like companies offered later. I think we missed something important that we both needed."

"We will work on it another time, and see if we can find ways to make it easier."

At the following session, I felt badly about Betsey's blank, distracted look. Slumped in the far corner of the room by the windows, she looked almost invisible on the light brown couch. Everything about her was unobtrusive: her hair, her drawn face, and her thin body in nondescript clothing.

She seemed far away, not with us at all. She reminded me of myself during a major depression, only she perked up a little when Dr. Smith asked her thoughts on subjects being discussed.

A gray-haired man close to my age joined us that day. He was thin, with tired-looking eyes and a little paunch. He told us he had been deeply depressed since losing, within a brief period of time, three people who had been close to him.

He shifted around in his chair, then said, "I eyed two closets, wondering whether to get them together." He was staring out the windows.

I said, "I don't understand."

"My gun was in one and the ammunition in the other."

The silence seemed electrical. Judging by myself, we were all stunned. We didn't question him. I thought he would continue if he felt able to disclose any more. It seemed quite apparent that in his profound grief he had contemplated suicide. Thank goodness, he decided against it.

When asked about my holiday upset, I shared the latest of several letters I'd written to the relative who had ruined my holiday dinner party.

Dr. Smith, frowning, leaned forward in his chair and said, "Don't send it. Your unsent letters have not resolved your anger, or the problem. What you need to do is discuss it with her."

A few days later I took his advice and told the relative, when invited to her home, "I can't stand to have anyone hurt my children. What happened at my dinner party made me angry, shaky, and almost in tears. I've had a terrible time dealing with it."

She hugged me and said, "I'm soooo sorry."

"Well, I am too, but I had to tell you how I felt." I gulped. "Now it's resolved. What's important is that we get along."

After we left I felt greatly relieved, brushed my hands together, and told Ralph, "There, that's taken care of."

Dorothy hurried in a few minutes late at the following meeting. She wore a full floral skirt, open-collared camp shirt that exposed her bountiful bosom, and high-heeled pumps, with no hosiery. She plopped down onto a couch and sighed. Soon after her arrival she started to rant and rave about her husband. We offered several suggestions. To mention a few, she was told:

"Get restraining orders."

"Tell the police, so your husband can't threaten or bother you."

Bill, a marine who had a terrible time expressing his feelings, said succinctly, "Leave."

Dorothy looked around at us with a menacing look and said, "You don't know what it's like. I'm not about to leave my home." I wondered why she had joined the group. She fought us all the way. She was as unreasonable as I had been when determined to go into business. That was it! It hadn't occurred to me that she was manic. How rough it was on anyone exposed to it!

"Now the lawyer wants more money because my case is so complicated," she said, heaving a sigh. "Everything's impossible."

That's confusing, I reflected, now she sounds more depressed than manic. I just can't figure her out

"What motivates you to live your life the way you do?" Dr. Gottlieb asked.

"I just want to be somebody."

Was that supposed to make sense? I asked myself, feeling more puzzled than ever.

Dorothy, scowling, again looked around at us, then said, "You're all mad at me. You tell me what to do, but you just don't understand."

Dr. Gottlieb reassured her that we did care. We showed it by urging her to get police protection and restraining orders.

Dr. Smith said, "I have an epitaph for Dorothy. 'I was right, even if it killed me.'"

To my amazement, she was silent. The session ended on a light note. Several of us muffled our snickers.

The following week, Dorothy told us she had been on private duty for a blind lady and had done far more than was required to help the family.

Then she said, with pursed lips, "After all that, the lady's husband bawled me out for abusing my telephone privileges. Can you beat that? I told him off and gave my two weeks notice."

She told us in detail how much she had done for him, how unfair he was, and how upset it made her. Her right leg jiggled at a rapid pace as she talked.

"So what happened?" someone asked.

"Would you believe this? He apologized and begged me to stay, and not to worry about the phone. He even gave me a fifty-cent an hour raise."

"That's great," we said in a chorus.

"What's so great about it? I'm still furious. He had a lot of nerve insulting me about the phone, after all I did."

"So you're not taking him up on his offer?" I said.

"Yeah, I decided to stay."

I shook my head, hoping to sort it all out.

As I looked at the others it struck me that the man with the gun problem had not returned to group. I presumed that his troubles were so severe that he had been hospitalized.

Arleen, the pregnant wife of a marine, said, "Dorothy, I'm glad you stood up for yourself and that it turned out well." The girl certainly didn't look pregnant, but her face was pale against her dark hair. She blinked a lot and absently rubbed her fingers. I hoped Dorothy wouldn't notice.

Dr. Smith pointed out that Dorothy tended to run when things didn't suit her. She must have tuned him out as usual, because she didn't react.

"I'm trying to learn," I said, "that although it's frustrating to displease someone no matter what I do, I have to value myself anyway. And another thing, I know I can't change anyone except myself, yet I keep trying to change Ralph. It's so maddening to have him know how much his shabby appearance bothers me, yet he won't do a darned thing about it. He refuses to get rid of any worn-out or outgrown clothes and persists in wearing them over and over. He even wears the same raggedy thing day after day."

Dr. Gottlieb said, "Is it easy to change yourself?"

"No. Nothing I value doing is easy."

"About your husband's clothes, does 'what will people think' enter it?"

I hesitated, then said, "Maybe partly, but he's such a good-looking man, I hate to have him look like a derelict."

"I like to wear old clothes and not shave when I'm not on duty," Bill said. "It feels good."

"When my husband's clothes get to me," Betsey said, "I put 'em in the trash." I was amazed at her audacity.

On the way home from group I told myself I should remember Ralph's good points and ignore what I disliked. I knew what I should do, but couldn't seem to do it. No doubt doing unto others was still good advice. I would try harder to give him the unconditional love we both longed to have.

At our next meeting Dorothy wore tight jeans and another camp shirt. Her hair looked particularly wild that day. She pointed out how nervous my fidgety fingers and feet made me look.

I said, "I'm usually not aware of it. I'd stop it if I could."

"Who does she remind you of, Charlotte?" Dr. Smith asked, motioning toward Dorothy.

"Mom, until she was almost ninety. She was hyper-critical of me. No matter what I did I could not please her. That's what made me feel as if I could not do anything right."

"Anyone else?"

I paused, then said, "Her remarks also remind me of the cameraman of a Suicide Prevention Program I was on. While filming it, the camera focused on my restless fingers twice. But I thought this was a place where we had no need to feel self-conscious, and could just be ourselves."

"I only meant to help you," said Dorothy, with a phoney smile and a sing-song voice like a taunting child.

I looked right at her, with narrowed eyes, "Frankly, I think you're being picky, not helpful." I refrained from asking her why she was so darned fat and looked like a slob.

To my amazement, she mentioned my hands again later. That time I was ready for her and said, "Yep, you're right. I'll have to do something about that."

I learned that in the Counseling Techniques Course, but sometimes forgot to apply it. I decided that if she jabbed me again

I'd say, "What do you suggest I do about it?"

Dr. Smith announced as we were leaving that after next week's meeting we would have to change to Tuesdays.

My reaction to Dorothy's criticism had made it an uncomfortable session for me, I thought as I walked to my car. There must be an easier way to learn the things I should know.

I became more than a little upset when Dorothy pointed out at our next meeting not only my fingers and feet, but what she called my "nervous laugh." Why on earth was she criticising me so much? She aimed all those remarks at me. I intensely disliked being her scapegoat. It made me feel both angry and self-conscious when she called everyone's attention to me, and again claimed, "I only meant to help you."

My head pounded with her words. I said, "Dammit anyway, you keep reminding me of my mom. There seems to be no way I can please you either."

Some of the group thought I overreacted. Maybe so, but at least I showed honest negative emotion instead of bottling it up. For me that was progress, even if it did sound defensive.

After I announced that I would be gone on a trip for three weeks, Dorothy said, "I think you ought to make an effort to not miss group for that long."

To my surprise, Bill spoke up and said, "I think Charlotte is a beautiful lady. I feel bad about her getting upset." That was the one time I heard him express his feelings.

"What a nice thing to say, Bill. Thank you." I gratefully smiled at him.

When I looked at Betsey, in her usual corner of the couch by the windows, she looked more withdrawn than usual. Her gaze was focused under Dr. Smith's chair. He always sat in the only armchair in the room. We saved it for him.

When Dr. Gottlieb tried to draw her out she said, "I've gone to a very private place. At one time I felt like leaving, but I didn't."

I wondered whether it was when Dorothy persisted in criticising me. When I became the butt of her attacks, other members may have felt as uncomfortable as I did. They were definitely more quiet than usual.

I jumped slightly as Dorothy struck again. "As a graduate from that school of charm and modeling," she taunted, "what did you do about your nervous habits?"

"What's the matter, Dorothy, do you get your kicks from putting me on the hot seat, or are you jealous?" I said in an elevated voice. Oh my, I had let her get to me again.

She ignored both questions. How I wished she'd get off my case.

On the way down the hall after group ended, I asked Dr. Smith, "How can I stop overreacting to criticism?"

"You have to untie the strings to the past," he said.

I simply had to learn how, either in group or during my private sessions with him.

Notes:

9

What a Relief

I am righteously indignant; you are annoyed; he is making a fuss about nothing.—Competition, New Statesman

"Dorothy won't be able to come to group on Tuesdays," Dr. Smith told us the following week. "She couldn't change her day off from work."

"Well, I have to admit that's a relief to me," I said.

Betsey said, "Me too."

Two new members were with us that day. Mike, a brawny marine non-com, who sat jiggling one leg up and down like a drum roll, looked as if he wished he could be somewhere else.

Madge, a voluptuous brunette, looked about twenty years younger than I, but older than Betsey. The corners of her lips twitched. Her attractive face was marred by scowls.

Mike mentioned his recent hospitalization, then said, "I'm on medication now and have learned a lot about my illness."

Dr. Smith said, "Would you care to share the nature of your disorder?"

"No, I'd rather not." He rubbed his hands up and down his

thighs and stared at a blank wall.

I said, "I'm manic-depressive, if that's any help."

He looked at me with raised eyebrows. "You are? I am too." He opened up about some of his problems due to the illness.

Madge's eyes looked frigid, and her mouth grim when she said, "I don't like all this talk about manic-depression. I'm *not* manic-depressive, but I'm so fed up with my life I almost succeeded in killing myself."

"I'm sorry," several of us said at once.

Mike said, "I know I talked about my illness quite a bit, but I haven't been able to before, and it sure was a relief."

I looked at Betsey. I hoped she would soon open up about her feelings. She was a sweet person who brought out my maternal instincts.

I openly shared my relief and feelings about Dorothy's being unable to come on Tuesdays. Dr. Smith walked over to me and patted my shoulder. He was so obviously pleased when we could express our feelings.

Madge became angry when Dr. Gottlieb introduced himself as Commander instead of Doctor.

"I can always tell when patients are mad at me," Dr. Smith said, "that's when they call me Captain, not Doctor."

I could not imagine getting mad at Dr. Smith, but perhaps some patients resented his authority.

"I hate rank," said Madge. "I hate officers. I hate this base." She glowered at us. Her hands became fists. "I hate the housing development where I live and the way the neighbors behave, and the gossip and violence, and the intrusions on my privacy and having nothing in common with anybody." She took a quick breath before continuing.

The room crackled with her fury.

"I hate having my husband re-up after telling me he was going to get out of the service." She took another breath. "And I hate the discrimination among officers' and enlisted men's children and wives."

Wow, I thought, that's the biggest outburst of anger I've heard in all the group sessions put together. She sounds as furious as I did at times when I was manic. Maybe more.

Madge went on to say, "All my troubles, and my daughter's, she's twelve, would be over if we could just live off the base. Of course my husband and his buddies would still talk about nothing but the military, and I might collect the same sort of neighbors until I learn how to handle that kind of people."

Our time was up. Madge's tirade reminded me of the many difficult people I've had to cope with. My collection included the siamese twins, hyper-sensitive and hyper-critical, and the self-righteous know-it-alls who insisted on telling me how to live my life.

Bill and I were the first to arrive at the following meeting. After everyone else got there, Bill said, "It might sound weird, but I feel uncomfortable when my wife acts real nice. I wonder why she's doing it. It's easier when she's bitchy. Then I can just say anything I feel like."

"That's funny," I said, "I'm just the opposite. I don't enjoy snapping and snarling one bit. It makes me feel awful."

"I feel like a complete failure," Mike, the non-com, said. His usually square shoulders sagged, and so did his rugged face.

"How can you?" I asked. "You've almost completed twenty years in the corps—and you've had a lot of promotions."

"I have so much trouble making decisions. But I do feel good," his face lit up, "about my decision to live off base, where I can have my dog. I made myself sick all week-end before I could finally decide."

"Mike," I said, "don't feel bad. When I was real depressed I couldn't decide the most insignificant things, like what to wear.

The decision you were wrestling with was an important one. You didn't give up. You ought to feel proud of yourself."

Several members agreed.

"About failure, I've failed in my marriage," Bill said. "I still love my wife, but I drove her away when I was manic."

"I think it's almost impossible for a marriage to survive manic-depression," I said, looking at Bill, "unless the spouse gets some help and understanding of the illness."

Dr. Gottleib said, "That's true. They need to seek help."

The following week, Betsey and I met on the elevator and walked to the room together. I told her how pretty she looked in her turquoise blouse and skirt. She smiled. I sat next to her on the couch.

I started the session by telling about a book I'd read, *Anger and Hurts.* "It said that hurts, anger, and irritation can come from our values and expectations, whether or not they are appropriate. "I get angry when people claim they know what I think, or they misinterpret something I said or did. What bothers me is that they are way off base. They make false accusations."

Betsey spoke up, "I have trouble relating to the girls I work with two nights a week. (I was stunned that she could work.) It's a great job, but I feel the age difference. Compared to them, I feel old. They don't take their work seriously at all. They just put in their time and could care less about the quality of their work. My folks taught me, 'If a job's worth doing, it's worth doing right.'"

We reassured her, but I wondered how she could feel old. She couldn't have been much more than thirty years old.

Dr. Gottleib said, "Betsey, I want to congratulate you on your progress in group participation."

When group was almost over she actually revealed that ten years ago she was raped. Tears made it difficult for her to speak. When she did, she said, "I still haven't gotten over it. My sex life's pretty good, but I just can't forget that horrible night."

I reached over and patted her knee.

"One of our daughters was raped," I said. "It revolted me to think anyone could do such a thing to someone I loved so much. The man followed her down the hall, and forced his way into her apartment. He tied her up and threatened her with a knife. She got married soon after that. She was too terrified to live alone. It was an awful marriage that didn't last."

Although it had happened years ago, I had trouble getting the words out, but I made myself continue.

"Another daughter was molested. She told us right away and we went to the police. The desk sergeant said, 'We've had no other complaints about him. Not only that, he's the city manager's brother-in-law.'

"Ralph said, 'I don't give a damn who he's related to, he molested my little girl and I'm complaining.'

"I was so furious that I fantasized about grabbing both of the bastards by the balls and twirling them 'round and 'round, then hurling them down a cliff into the ocean."

Bill said, "They oughta have those things cut off. They should never be able to use 'em again."

Only three of us attended the following meeting. Dr. Smith had returned and Dr Gottleib was not there. I definitely preferred Dr. Smith. He was much more warm and perceptive. He encouraged us and injected a little humor at times. All in all I felt far more comfortable with him.

Betsey and I welcomed Red after a brief absence from the group. Like Bill, he often had trouble expressing his feelings, and they both had marital problems. Dr. Smith arrived and welcomed him too.

Red reversed his chair, straddled it, leaned his arms on the back and announced, "My wife and I have separated."

We groaned sympathetically.

"We've had a lot of trouble communicating," he continued. "I still admire her a lot, but thought I should get myself together before we tried to resume our marriage." He gulped before being able to go on.

"She went through hell while I was in the active stage of this illness, so I sent her away." His hands thrummed on his thighs. "She's delayed signing the divorce papers, but wants to know where she can reach me twenty-four hours a day. I don't want to be that available."

He sounded a little mixed up to me, yet I was pleased that he could talk that much. I hoped he and his wife could straighten everything out when they were both ready.

"So now," Red shifted his long legs, "I want a taste of doing what I want to do when I want to do it—with no personal demands. I've discovered books, and want to read during all my spare time."

Betsey said, "My husband and I got so we could tease each other a lot. It's been fun. He used to think all women, including me, were cheaters."

"Was his mother a cheater?" I asked.

"How did you know?"

"People often generalize because of something painful that happened to them."

"I had a problem ten years ago," said Betsey, "that's been on my mind a lot lately."

Dr. Smith said, "Would you like to tell us about it?"

"No, I ... I can't. Her face was averted. "Didn't Dr. Gottleib tell you about last week?"

"No."

With a little supportive encouragement, she was able to acknowledge to Dr. Smith that she had been raped.

Dr. Gottleib said, "It sometimes helps to walk through a problem."

"What does that mean?" Betsey said.

"It means," Dr. Smith said, "look at it a step at a time and get the feelings out, so it can be resolved."

"I'm not sure I want all the ah ... discomfort or, oh I don't know the word."

"Pain?" I asked, and she agreed.

"Would it make it go away for sure?" Betsey looked at Dr. Smith.

"No promises, but it often does."

"Would it be easier in a private session?"

"That's your choice, Betsey, but you can be sure the group would be supportive."

He turned to Red and asked him how he felt about this. I was flabbergasted when he both intellectualized at length and defended men in general. I started to squirm in my seat.

"I notice that Charlotte has some feelings about this," Dr. Smith said.

"I sure do. It really upsets me. I can't see how anyone can intellectualize about a thing like that. It's one of the worst things that can happen to a girl or woman and I feel sickened for Betsey. Rape is a terrible trauma. Our daughter who was raped had to have therapy to get over it."

"Charlotte, what would you do if you were raped?" Dr. Smith asked.

"After reporting it to the police and seeing a doctor, I'd call you and say, 'You've gotta help me. I can't handle this alone.'"

Betsey appeared stricken as she looked at me and said, "I should have gotten help long ago."

"But you can't do anything about that, Betsey. Get the help now," I urged.

After the others left, Betsey stayed there on the couch next to me. She looked drained.

I reached over and gently patted her arm, then asked, "Want to walk down to the elevator with me, or would you like to have me stay here with you?"

"I think I'll just sit here for a while. You run along."

"All right. I just want you to know how much I care. See you next week."

At the next session we all sat in our usual places. We were joined by a pale, short, compactly built marine. His hair was cut even more closely than that of the other marines. I had heard it called a "high shave" and could see why. His arm was in a sling.

When asked to tell us about himself, he said, "My name's Eddie, I'm twenty-two, have a communication problem, and I never finish things I start, like courses, hobbies, and interests. Oh, and I have to have everything controlled or structured."

Later he said, "I'm really inhibited about talking to people. I have to plan what I'll say and figure out what they'll say. Then I wonder what they meant by what they said. I don't dare share a problem with friends because they joke about it when I do."

"That's a darn shame," I said. "You miss so much, like spontaneous talk and good-natured fun, and shared confidences."

Betsey, who had been gazing at the floor, said, "If I work on my big problem privately, Dr. Smith, how does that work?"

"What do you mean? How do you want it to work?"

"I'd like you and Dr. Gottleib and Charlotte to be with me. Could that be done?"

I was both overwhelmed and deeply touched.

"Well, yes, we could work something out. We'll get together next week and set up a time." Betsey looked relieved.

Dr. Smith then asked Eddie how he felt about being there.

"Uncomfortable. I feel as if I'm in the spotlight being watched and analyzed." He looked at the wall out of the corner of his eyes.

I said, "I know what you mean about the spotlight and the watching, but we aren't critical. Sometimes it helps us to know we're not the only ones with certain feelings. It's less lonely. If we can say something helpful, it makes us feel good too. We develop a real caring for each other here."

With his head cocked to one side and his brows furrowed, Dr. Smith said, "I have mixed emotions about Eddie. We were just getting to know him, then he told us he has trouble finishing things he starts."

Eddie looked down while alternately crossing his legs.

After a second or two Red said, "I've been having a lot of stomach trouble lately, so I didn't go to my communication class at college. We were having a test."

I wondered whether the pending test upset his stomach or whether his upset stomach made his miss the test.

He also revealed that he, like Eddie, had become aware that control was extremely important to him.

"What about your feelings?" Dr. Smith asked.

No response.

"Charlotte, have you noticed any of Red's feelings?"

"None. He's kind of like a robot."

Eddie sat in his chair looking around the room as if he might be finding everything a little boring, or uncomfortable.

I sat there thinking how much Eddie and Red valued self-control. Close relationships must be almost impossible for them, and the fun that comes from spontancity.

"Next Tuesday's my birthday," I said as we were closing, so I'm not sure I'll be here."

"You could celebrate Monday," Dr. Smith said.

"That's an idea. See you next week."

At the following meeting we all arrived at once. Red told us he felt real confused. He had been intolerant and aggressive about waiting in line for a hamburger. "I have a problem when I feel manipulated." His jaw dropped, his eyes widened, then he hung his head and said, "I'm a manipulator myself."

After a pause he then went on to say, "I've changed my mind about reuniting my family I can't put my wife through any more, and our son is victimized by the whole situation." He stared at his hands, clasped between his knees.

Betsey looked at Red and said, "In spite of my terrible tantrums, my son wants to be with me." She might not say much, I thought, but when she did she came up with some gems.

"I wonder why so many of us have trouble expressing our negative feelings," I said. "I've decided that I'm afraid I won't get approval, or will be rejected." Everyone was quiet. I wondered whether they disapproved of what I said, or were trying the idea on for size.

Eddie broke the silence. "I have a lot of stress. Normally I run to get calmed down, but I haven't done it lately and can't do push-ups or pull-ups until this arm is better."

"I run," Bill said.

Both Red and Eddie said they had to have extra sleep to help cope with stress. And escape their feelings? I asked myself. "I get out of a lot of things because of stomach troubles," Red told us.

Like the test at college? I wondered.

"I'm discouraged," he continued, "in fact, I feel pretty hopeless about not responding to lithium, and about my problems."

I said, "I guess I've been real lucky with lithium, and thought most people were. But I share your problem about stress. I have to learn ways to deal with it."

"About sharing problems," Eddie said, "the last people I could share them with are my folks. They're in Phoenix anyway, but when we're together I never hug my mom or even shake hands with my dad." He ran his hand around the nape of his neck.

Dr. Smith asked, "Would you care to share your feelings about your parents?"

"No, I'd rather not. I can't."

"I often feel like a puppet with my mom," I told him.

"Try to express your feelings to her," Dr. Smith advised. "For instance, say, 'When you talk like that I feel ....' Or say, 'Well, I have to go. I'll come again soon when you're in a better mood, or feel better.'"

"Why couldn't I think of that?" I asked. "I'll try it."

Later, Betsey mentioned that in two weeks she planned to take a three-week visit. She added, "About the ... the rape. I'll wait till the subject comes up easily." She was looking at the floor.

That floor drew a lot of attention, I thought. Poor Betsey. I suspected that she wasn't ready to talk about it yet, or to have our four-way appointment, but the timing had to be right for her. Her wearing brighter clothes today had made me hope she was finally able to work on what she called her "big problem."

10
Who's Pulling My Strings?

The prejudiced and obstinate man does not so much hold opinions, as his opinions hold him.—Tryon Edwards

The following week, after we all settled into our seats, Dr. Smith began the discussion. He sat up in his chair, instead of lounging like he usually did.

"Manic-depression is a genetic disease," he said, "but not everyone in the family gets it. If I had to have a mental illness, I would choose manic-depression."

The room was hushed. Perhaps the others were as startled as I. After a brief pause he continued, "It is incurable, but the most treatable mental illness."

"Really?" and "No fooling?" were all that we managed to say. After giving us a few moments to absorb what he said, he asked, "Would any of you like to tell about your symptoms?"

Everyone else was silent, so I said, "My mood swings were extreme, but when deeply depressed, no matter how sad I felt, I couldn't cry."

"Mine were pretty extreme too," Betsey told us, "but I could hardly stop crying."

Several of us told about our incapacitating depressions, marked by the classic symptoms of sleepless nights, painful indecision, and suicide attempts. Repeatedly, I noted surprise and relief on my peers' faces as they found out that many of their own symptoms were typical of the illness. It must have been a great relief to each one of us, not only me, to realize that our misery was not unique. We were not alone after all.

We talked about our manic episodes, when non-stop talking, angry outbursts, and hyperactivity took over. I said, "I had a temporary job at a large firm. I brought in a small radio for my office and a bowl of jelly beans to offer my co-workers. My over-inflated opinion of both my position and my capabilities was laughable later, yet embarrassing. I overheard a couple of young women who worked there say, "Who does she think she is, bringing in a radio? None of the rest of us has ever had one."

Red tilted back in his chair and said, "After hearing you folks talk, I guess I haven't had it so bad."

My gaze wandered over to Betsey, who looked more alert than usual. "Luckily for me," she said, "my husband kids around a lot when something terrible happens, like when we had an intruder on our property. Joe has a great sense of humor. It has helped me get over a lot of uncomfortable situations."

She looked pretty that day, with her new hairstyle that did not cover her eyes. Because she had taken a step to improve her appearance, I concluded that she must be feeling better.

I said, "Your husband creates a nice diversion. I would like that."

Bill mentioned that when he had asked earlier how I was, I did not sound like myself.

"Probably because Ralph and I had an argument just before I came in. He couldn't find his shirt for exercise class this morning. I told him I noticed that it smelled gamey and had put it in the dirty clothes.

"Then he said, 'That's the only one I had. When's the last time you washed?'

"I felt attacked and said, 'If you would just stop talking to me as if you were commanding the troops! You know I wash every two weeks because you want me to save energy.'

"He was silent, but I was still ticked off and asked, 'Aren't you ever going to learn to hang up your clothes, or put 'em in the clothes hamper when they're dirty? If you did, you'd know where they were.' That ended the argument."

The group crackled with suggestions:

Eddie said, "Why don't you stuff his shirt in his pillow or his shoe?"

Someone else thought I should never pick up his clothes, but let him dress as he pleased and ignore how he looked.

One marine said, "You don't have to be the good wife and take care of him. If you react to his fury, he'll dish it out."

I thought that was terrific. Don't react to his fury. I would have to remember that

"Just quietly leave the room when he starts in on you," someone else said.

"I think you were right when you told him to pick up his own clothes, then he'd know where they were."

Dr. Smith said, "Try to stop being both the 'good girl' and Miss Perfect for a week and see what happens. Ask yourself who is pulling your strings."

Oh no, I thought, don't tell me I'm still caught up in that role.

I hated to, but had to say, "I can't be here next week. My former bridge club was desperate to have me substitute. I agreed to do it that one time."

Everyone laughed. Did they think I was trying to get out of doing my homework? Oh well, it was fun to leave with laughter echoing in my ears.

When I returned to group two weeks later, I was asked to share my assignment. I had written it out so I could read it to the others:

THE GOOD GIRL/MISS PERFECT PROBLEM
or WHO'S PULLING MY STRINGS?

1. At the commissary Ralph said, "Want these little carrots in our cart?"

"Yes, that's why I put them there."

"They're sure expensive."

"They're sweet little baby carrots I planned to have for company." I began to feel defensive.

"I just wanted to be sure you knew what you were doing."

"I do." One thing I was doing was getting mad, but I didn't want to make a scene. I choked back my feelings and asked him to look for some cookies so I could shop for something else in peace.

2. People have at times tried to force me to accept their religious beliefs. One person in particular insisted that I go to the church she was enthused about at the time. She had switched from one to another and was equally enthusiastic about each one.

I reluctantly went with her the first time. She was extremely persuasive. Everything was radically different from anything I had ever been exposed to. It made me feel uncomfortable. I wondered what I was doing there.

The next time she was carried away about her current church, I was able to truthfully say, "No, I'm sorry, but my own church gives me just what I need." Well, come to think of it, I wasn't really sorry. It was a relief to be able to have the courage of my convictions.

3. Being asked repeatedly to join a person's pet affiliation makes me equally uncomfortable. I dislike being urged to join anything in which I have no interest.

4. Since Ralph retired I have desperately needed some time to myself, but have been unable to have

any. He makes plans to be gone whenever I am gone. When I stay home, he does too. Retirement and an overdose of togetherness have been the pits so far, but what can I do?

5. Mother was an expert at pulling my strings. As conservator of both her finances and physical care I had endless responsibilities. I did not mind that. Without a doubt, she needed the help.

What bothered me was her insistence that we visit her on Sundays, rather than any other time. It was not always convenient. When Ralph and I took two-week trips, even though our daughter Cathi visited her while we were gone, Mother complained—and it stirred up my guilt.

6. Something that *really* bothers me is to receive French kisses from the unexpected and inappropriate source of friends or acquaintances.

When I finished reading, Dr. Smith moved forward in his chair and asked, "How do you feel about letting other people pull your strings?"

I squirmed around a little, then said, "I don't like it one little bit. Looks as if I have to refuse to do things I don't want to do, even though others expect me to do them."

"Anything else?"

"When it bothers me, I have to express how I feel about what people say or do."

It occurred to me, on the way home, that I had just leaped over an emotional hurdle. I felt a warm glow.

 *Notes:*

11

Unexpressed Feelings

He that will not apply new remedies must expect new evils.
— Bacon

Eddie was the last to straggle into the meeting the following week. I felt concerned about how forlorn he looked. His shoulders sagged. His face had about as much expression as a cigar store Indian's.

After getting Dr. Smith's okay, I asked Eddie whether he was depressed.

"Yes, I'm always depressed."

"That must be terrible. When I had major depressions it was impossible to make decisions of any kind. I just wanted to be alone, because I was so self-conscious. Besides, I had no energy."

He didn't answer, but looked as if he were listening.

Encouraged, I continued. "It was real difficult to make a phone call, or even answer the phone."

Later I said, "I had shock treatments that ended my last depression in five weeks instead of two months. I've had no more mood swings for years, thank goodness, but every morning I lay out my daily medication so I'll be sure I've taken it. I made up my mind I'd never go through a depression again, if I could prevent it."

Eddie jiggled his leg. "I forget to take mine most of the time. I even forget my appointments with Dr. Smith." He stared bleakly out the window. When he talked I had to lean forward to hear him.

"What does your illness bring you, Eddie?" Dr. Smith asked.

"I guess it helps me run away."

The room was silent for seconds that seemed like minutes. Then Ruth, a stylishly dressed blonde, changed the subject. She had come to group for the first time. "I worry an awful lot about our three adult children. It's gotten out of hand lately. I need help."

For a while we discussed the importance of expressing her feelings, which seemed to be involved in her problem.

"After years of trying," I said, "I still have trouble expressing my negative feelings. I can only do it once in a while, not nearly as often as I need to."

Red spoke up. "Why don't you practice telling a powerful person how you really feel? Maybe you should just tell it like it is."

Appalled at the thought, I gasped. "I can't imagine doing that. I was taught to be polite."

"What's the matter? Afraid you'll hurt people's feelings? Maybe their feelings don't get hurt as easily as yours. Some people are real aggressive. You have to stand up for yourself."

"Okay, I'll think about it. But something that upsets me even more is when people are over-solicitous. They act as if I might get sick any minute if I've been under a little stress. Another thing that bugs me is being treated like a child. Ralph does that sometimes. Questioning everything I do insults my intelligence, so does over-explaining. I've told him how I feel about those things, but he keeps on doing it."

Later, I wondered whether I changed the subject to avoid discomfort.

Dr. Smith said, "There's only one way to win an argument, and that is to express your feelings." He made so many astute observations, yet in an unassuming way.

We heard the words, "Express your feelings," repeatedly in that barren, though often emotionally charged room.

I told myself firmly that I MUST form a habit of expressing my negative feelings. That would be my new goal. With practice it should get easier, like saying "please" or "thank-you."

Dr. Gottleib caught my attention when he said, "Charlotte, what would make you happy?"

Before I could answer, the discussion veered off in another direction.

As we walked out the door I told him, "I heard your question. I'll let you know next week."

That afternoon I again wrote out my thoughts and put the paper in my purse, ready to share. It said:

WHAT WOULD MAKE ME HAPPY?

1. Handle the puppeteers in my life so well that they would stop pulling my strings. If they did nothing about their own problems, they would have to find new puppets.

2. Express my feelings in mature, productive ways. Say, when necessary, "I'm sorry, but I can't do that."

3. Overcome my sensitivity, anger, and frustration whenever any of those emotions are excessive or inappropriate.

4. Feel important, no matter what anyone says or does.

5. Tell people, without trying to change them, how I feel about their actions or words.

Writing it made me realize once more that my feelings must be expressed, so I could put an end to being dominated or manipulated by others. The list, as I reread it, was thought-provoking. I felt certain that the changes, though challenging, were essential to both my emotional and physical health, and to my happiness.

Eddie was obviously not depressed the following week. He said, "I've really goofed with my lithium medication. Figured out it was because I had doubts about wanting to get well."

"And I've always taken mine compulsively, I said, because I was afraid that if I didn't I might get manic or depressive again."

Red was scowling when he said, as if unaware of our discussion, "I'm going back east next month and try to get my family together again. Sounds like my son's starting to show signs of the illness. I gotta help him."

We expressed our concern and let him know we admired him for trying to help.

May, a gray-haired woman new to the group, told us she had anxiety attacks and recurrent depression, but adjusted her medication (not lithium) because it made her sleepy.

I couldn't imagine doing that unless instructed to by the physician monitoring the medication.

She had no interests and a terrible fear of losing her husband, who had a heart condition. They lived an extremely limited lifestyle, with no balance of activity.

Nobody said anything. As I looked around the circle I surmised that, like me, they were listening but could not think of anything to say. That happened sometimes.

I broke the silence, saying, "Dr. Smith, can anyone recover from manic-depression?"

"It is an incurable mental illness, but the most treatable one."

A few of us had heard that before, but I wondered whether research had brought any change. Besides, it might help the current group to hear about it, since our membership revolved.

After we had time to digest his answer to my question Dr. Smith asked, "Does anyone here know Eddie?" He has been with us for several weeks."

The young marine mentioned immediately began to twist and turn in his chair, and to look at the floor.

Several people said, "Nope."

"He's extremely anxious and hates Food Service," one of the marines said. "He was expected to be a high achiever and he has blanked out a lot of his childhood years."

"I've blanked out my earlier years too," said Red. Then he talked to Eddie quite a bit about the corps. He wound up saying, "They sure do assign us a lot of shitty jobs; they have to be done too, whether we like it or not."

I told Eddie, "Ralph had a lot of rough jobs he didn't enjoy in the service, but I've heard him say, 'I just figured that was the breaks.'"

It seemed to me Eddie had trouble coping with anything that didn't work out the way he wanted it to. He sure needed to know that it was impossible to control everything in life. If he was that inflexible at twenty-two, what would he be like as he grew older? Like Dr. Smith had implied at an earlier meeting, I hoped he would not give up on psychological help like he had on other things.

When we stopped discussing Eddie's problems I said, "It seems futile to tell Ralph how much it bothers me to have to ride in his Pinto on hot days like today. Unlike our other car, it has no air-conditioning. Yet the newer one, with all its comforts, sits in our driveway.

"He said, 'I drove it today so we could pick up the new screen door you thought you had to have.'

"I wouldn't have been so mad if he'd told me in advance, but he keeps insisting that we go places in that old car. When I told him before how I felt about the Pinto I was glad I said it, but it doesn't matter to him—not one bit. I know I can't change him, but I'm so damned tired of being the only one who works on our problems."

Dr. Smith said, "Do you let other people's anger rule you?"

I thought for a second. "Yes, I guess so. Lately, I've expressed my feelings much more often, but when it's seems obvious that I'm talking to a closed, bolted door, I give up."

A little later I asked, "How can I cope with manipulation? That's a big hang-up for me."

Again the doctor said, "Express your feelings."

Evidently it was therapeutic, I told myself, even when the

desired results weren't apparent. I'd have to persist in my efforts.

Everyone had looked intrigued when Dr. Smith and I briefly discussed manipulation.   Too bad it was time to leave.

On the way home I wondered whether I should have told Eddie something I had heard about flexibility; it is important to be flexible, so you will never be bent out of shape.

When I reached home, I looked up "manipulation" in my Webster's dictionary. Definitions included: "to manage or control artfully or by shrewd use of influence, especially in an unfair ... way."

A brief research revealed that manipulating, or pulling other people's strings, was often done by alcoholics, drug addicts, and bullies. It was done more subtly by chronic complainers, bores, interrupters, and strongly opinionated persons. That last category was the one that had caused me the most trouble.

I vowed that I would find ways to deal with manipulation, and with the people who pulled my strings.

12

Time to Move On

Vice, virtue, and time are three things that never stand still.
— Colton

Betsey was the last to arrive at the meeting. She was greeted by whistles when she walked in, after returning from a family reunion in the midwest. Her light brown hair was cut shorter and restyled. She held her head high. Her azure blue dress intensified the blue of her eyes.

Ruth opened our discussion. She said, while wringing her hands, "My youngest daughter worries me. She has scarcely any money, and two daughters to take care of. I've given her six hundred dollars or so a month for a long time, but I finally stopped. I'm trying to let go." A frown creased her brow; her face appeared to be etched by worry.

Both Betsey and I urged her to release her daughters to live their own lives, even if they did have to struggle.

"I'm glad you're backing off," I added, " because most of us feel too obligated if our parents have been overly helpful."

"Or anyone else," Betsy added.

"Yes. Our eldest daughter told me Kahlil Gibran had made an interesting point when he wrote in *The Prophet* that parents are bows that send forth their children as living arrows."

"That had never occurred to me." Ruth rubbed her hands.

I mentioned that many wives lose their husbands after putting them through college.

Ruth moaned and said, "You have given me a lot to think about. Thank you."

Red, apparently absorbed in his own thoughts while slumped in his chair, said, "I still plan to join my family and bring them back here with me." In spite of his words, he looked the picture of dejection.

"My wife's giving me a lot of resistance," he said. "If only she could understand manic-depression." His mouth drooped.

Ruth asked Dr. Smith, "Would you write a letter to help my husband understand my illness? Maybe you could say, 'I know how upsetting Ruth's illness has been, and how rough it's been on you. She wasn't the same person when she was manic.'"

"Charlotte," Dr. Smith said, "have you told your husband that?"

"Yes, I have," I said thoughtfully, "and I think it helped, except I still hope I've heard the last of his resentment about my moving out one time. It was during a manic episode. He never could accept it, even after knowing more about my illness. He took it as a personal rejection."

Dr. Gottlieb called attention to Eddie, whose arm was still in a sling, and brought up how little he let us know him.

"I'm uncomfortable in any group—always have been," he said, licking his lips.

"I'd like to have you tell each member of the group how you feel about them."

He glanced at each of us in turn, after looking at the floor, then out the windows. "Well, I feel as if Ruth's real maternal.

"Red ought to throw himself at his wife's feet after telling her, 'You had your way; now I'm going to get mine.' Seems to me it's her turn to manipulate.

"Betsey and Charlotte talk, but it's like I don't hear them."

In spite of what he said about me, I couldn't help feeling sorry for him. He was so uncomfortable that he could not look us in the eye. He made it clear that he had difficulty with relationships.

"To me, the doctors," Eddie continued, "represent authority, so I feel like I need to look and sound good."

On the way out after the session ended, I caught up with Dr. Smith and said, "I'd like to graduate from group. I think the others are a lot sicker than I am. Believe me, I feel luckier than ever to have those mood swings under control."

"Why don't you talk to them about it next week?"

I sighed. "Well, okay. See you next week."

Bill was at the following meeting. He's the one who had defended me against Dorothy when she kept on criticizing me. Betsey was gone.

Ruth apologized for talking so much the last time we met. She wore a black check pant suit with a black turtle neck blouse. She was always well-groomed and nicely dressed; quite a contrast to Dorothy, I thought.

"Don't feel bad," I told Ruth. "We seem to take turns talking more than usual. A few people are more silent than others, especially when depressed, but apologies are not necessary."

"I've been reading up on depression and anxiety," she said. "I'd like to ask you some questions, Dr. Smith."

"I'm sorry, Ruth, we can't do that in group."

I wondered why not, but that made private sessions even more valuable. I had to see him four times a year anyway to have my lithium treatment monitored; I would save my own questions until then.

"Tell me, how do you feel about Dr. Gottlieb?" Dr. Smith was still looking at Ruth.

"Last week I thought he treated me like he would an inattentive student," she replied. "When I was obviously not listening, he asked me what someone had said. It made me uncomfortable."

"I used to think he was mean," Red said, "but then his personality overcame it."

I said, "I have felt as if he quite often misinterpreted my remarks," then I turned toward him. "Now, Dr. Gottlieb, it's your turn to sit on the hot seat."

"You seem to be having trouble with authority figures, Charlotte."

"That isn't surprising. I sure have trouble with the authority figure I married. On the way to group I told Ralph I would like to get an air-conditioner for our home. I suffer so darned much from the heat. Why shouldn't I be able to be comfortable?

"He said, 'You just want one because your friend Marge has one.'"

"That made me mad. It was a false accusation. 'Marge has nothing to do with it. I want one because the heat wipes me out. It isn't as if we couldn't afford it.'

"After a stony silence he said, 'We didn't have one in our condo in Torrance.'

"'That's right, and I had to haul a fan around with me wherever I went. I see no reason to have to do that now. If it's the money that's bothering you, I'll pay for it myself. I simply want to be comfortable.'

"He didn't say a word, which infuriated me. How could I discuss something important when he was either prejudiced against it or mute?"

Red said, "Married people sure have trouble unless they have a partnership. Why don't you just have the air-conditioning put in? That seems to be his idea of a partnership. He does what he wants about money, so you do what you want, or handle part of the money yourself."

"Well, he's managed the money all his life. He prides himself on how far he makes it go. He was an authority figure in both his military and civilian jobs. His idea of a partnership is that he provides the money and is in charge of it, and I'm in charge of the household and social arrangements." I bit my lip.

Red said, "I think," he narrowed his eyes, "a lot of your problems with him are because you let him make all the important decisions."

"True, but I don't always do it without a fuss. While we were raising our kids I went along with his constant excuse, 'We can't afford it.' Now I know we can. I asked him to show me his accounting books. He justifies his decisions, but although I disagree, there seems to be no way to get him to change his mind. I've been submissive to keep the peace that I crave, or if I assert myself we have an exhausting power struggle. I don't want him to dominate me any longer. Now I realize it's also called pulling my strings, or manipulation."

"But can't you put your foot down when it's important?"

"I've tried everything I can think of, as well as other people's suggestions. He either gets mad or clams up. Maybe I just have to remember his assets—he has lots of those—and compliment him more. You made some good points, Red. Maybe I can put 'em together with other things I've learned here and get this thing resolved."

As we were closing I said, "I'd like to know how to transfer out of this outfit."

They laughed at my using a popular military expression. As we left they all shook hands with me.

While walking down the hall I asked Dr. Smith, "Is this how we terminate?"

"Usually you share your feelings, and the group does too."

"Oh. Then I'll see you next week."

When we met the following week Dr. Gottlieb said, "What are you doing here, Charlotte?"

"Dr. Smith told me the usual way to terminate was to talk about it in group."

I was disappointed that he was not at my final session. I preferred him to Dr. Gottlieb. I still thought he was a far more sensitive psychotherapist, one who offered more help and caring. If I had known he would not be there, I wouldn't have been either.

A new girl was with us, Helen, a disheveled, tall, thin young girl with long blonde hair. She said she was depressed and manic-depressive. I soon realized that her depression was not as extreme as the ones that had incapacitated me.

She said, "I was on lithium a few years ago, but went off it. I'm married, have a baby seven months old, and I'm pregnant." She looked at her hands as she massaged them.

In time she also told us, "My husband and I just arrived here from Quantico. We have money problems, so I'm trying to get a part-time job. I've got an interview today."

She amazed me. When I was depressed I couldn't possibly have said or done what she was doing.

"My sister arrives tomorrow to live with us," Helen said, as she gazed at the wall. It struck me that those blank walls received as much attention as the floor.

"She's manic-depressive too, but lithium finally made her well."

She may have felt better, I thought, but since manic-depression is incurable, she could not be free of the mood swings without her medication.

Helen continued, "My husband's a corporal. He has to go out in the field until Christmas time."

Her story made me realize that my current troubles were, by comparison, annoyances. I said, "I should think *anyone* with your problems would be depressed. I'm manic-depressive and have survived five years of extreme mood swings. Thanks to lithium I have been free of symptoms since 1973, but I have to take my medication the rest of my life."

Eddie said, "I'm manic-depressive. I finally decided to take my lithium, but lots of times I forget. I try to keep busy."

"You astonish me, Helen," I said. "When I was depressed I couldn't make the slightest decisions, and had absolutely no energy."

Dr. Gottlieb said, "We can't tell people what they should do when they aren't able to do it." I didn't think we were. We just told her about taking our lithium and how our illness affected us.

"When I went to a psychologist," Ruth said, "he told me what to do, but wouldn't help me because he said I wasn't doing anything to help myself."

"That's terrible," I said. "Why wouldn't he know that in the acute stage of the illness we can't possibly help ourselves? During those years I couldn't even think straight."

Someone said, "That's right. Me too."

"I think we're so lucky," I said, "to be able to get the wonderful care that we receive here."

"I have to have some blood tests today," Helen said, "have a job interview at 1:00, then pick up my son, and later my husband. And I have to at least unpack the room my sister will use. It's so full of boxes she won't be able to go to bed until they're cleared out."

"Try to be patient with yourself," I told her. "I know the treatment here will help you feel better, even if it may not look that way to you now."

Dr. Gottlieb told her about how much the group cared.

I took another chance on Eddie's listening to me. I told him again how I organized my lithium by putting the daily amount in a special place to take with my meals, so I'd be sure I had taken the prescribed amount each day.

A little later I announced with glee, "We're getting air-conditioning."

"You must have expressed your feelings," someone said.

"Yep, I asserted myself again about my need for comfort, because it was supposed to get up to 100 degrees. Then the darned fog made a liar out of me." They snickered. "I'm going to try to laugh at the aggravating things I used to take so seriously. Life's too short."

"That's a good, mature idea," Dr. Gottlieb said.

"Thanks, but I need to find a way to handle holiday problems better than I did last Christmas. If anyone gets out of line again I've gotta take them aside and express my feelings, rather than dwell on their awful behavior for days."

Helen began to talk again, looking distraught, "I can't take lithium because I'm pregnant. Abortion was recommended, but I'm not about to do that. Oh, and my seven-month-old needs correction on his feet. The appointment for that is next Tuesday, so I can't come to group."

Dr. Gottlieb said, "You could change your pediatric appointment and give the group priority."

I hoped she could take a day at a time and be stabilized soon. Then I looked at my watch. Time was running out, so I said, "Last week Dr. Gottlieb asked me what would make me happy. After a lot of thought, I decided it boiled down to being able to stop letting people pull my strings."

He said, "I like that answer. It sounds as if you've started to do it."

"Thank you," I said. "I'm graduating from the group today. I don't think I need it any more, but I'll continue to see Dr. Smith four times a year for my lithium treatment. I'll miss each one of you, and wish I knew how things were going for you, like Red's family, Eddie's arm and career, Ruth's life, and Helen's problems."

It was time to move on, to "go for it" with the new knowledge and awareness gained through the group experience.

I felt both sad and glad. What would I discover in the future? For me, that was what life was all about.

PART III

INSIDE
MANY FACETS
OF MOOD DISORDERS

13

Lithium, Physicians, and Marriage

Marriage is not like the hill of Olympus, wholly clear, without clouds.—Fuller

Dr. Smith monitored my lithium treatment for another year or more, and I continued to learn many valuable things from him.

He told me four reasons why many patients discontinued taking lithium:

1. They won't accept the fact that they have an incurable mental illness.
2. They don't want to have to depend on medication for the rest of their lives.
3. They refuse to take their medication as directed.
4. They will not give up their enjoyable highs.

It seemed incomprehensible to me that manic-depressive patients would avoid whatever it took to put them back in charge of their lives. The alternatives held no appeal for me. I had suffered more than enough of the misery the mood swings brought to both me and my family.

What worked for me was to accept the fact that I had a major mental illness, gratefully receive the treatment that controlled the symptoms, then do my part as a responsible patient. Those attitudes and actions freed me from a life sentence of bizarre thinking and behavior.

After treatment began, which in my case included psycho-therapy and medication, it was essential that I do my part. That meant that I was responsible for keeping my appointments with my physician, have my prescriptions filled as required, and take my medication on a regular basis. In addition, I must have blood tests ordered by the physician monitoring the lithium level, to be sure it remained within the therapeutic range.

Those things require a minimum of effort, yet that effort means the difference between a life of hell and a normal, productive, happy life.

When Dr. Smith had a new assignment, I had to find another psychiatrist. Dr. Thomas A. Flanagan was highly recommended by my lawyer. Several of his clients had sung the physician's praises. I could readily see why.

Dr. Flanagan, tall, handsome, and prematurely gray-haired, quickly demonstrated that he was a skilled physician who cared about his patients. His professional manner was softened by his warmth, and an occasional flicker of shyness. I liked him immediately, and was happy to have him monitor my lithium maintenance.

I have seen him every three months since 1985, a welcome improvement from having to change physicians so often. He called me Mrs. Clark until recently, when I said, "Don't you think you know me well enough by now to call me Charlotte?"

He grinned and said, "All right, Charlotte."

One day while discussing lithium, the magic answer for my illness, he startled me. Looking at me with his clear blue eyes he said, "You are one of the lucky ones."

I raised my eyebrows. "What do you mean, lucky? I thought most manic-depressives responded well to lithium."

He crossed his legs and turned slightly in his swivel chair. "Many patients have side effects that preclude their taking it."

"Oh my, I feel sorry for them. At the same time I feel really grateful that I've been so lucky."

Another thing I learned from Dr. Flanagan was that I should not hesitate to call him right away if I ever had a frightening side effect.

One day, after shaking inside and out, I did just that. He had me come right in, gave me instructions, then said, "Now don't you worry about this, we'll work it through together. Feel free to call me any time. If you need to see me, we'll work you in." His words were as comforting as a child's security blanket.

I thanked him, feeling sure that everything would soon be under control. It was, after a laboratory test, followed by a change in the amount of my medication. I felt luckier than ever, having that kind of support.

During one appointment, I told Dr. Flanagan about an argument with Ralph. He advised, "If you react to what he says or does, tell him how it makes you feel. Do not attack or defend. You might say, 'That hurts,' rather than, 'You're mean.' Do not provoke his anger by accusing him."

"Wait a minute. I have to get this down." I took notes so I wouldn't forget something important.

When I nodded that I was ready, he continued, "Take responsibility for your own feelings and reactions."

In different words, Dr. Smith had urged the members of the group to express our feelings. Having two highly respected physicians say the same thing added even more impact to their words.

In contrast, I remembered how upset I had been years back, when two surgeons had conflicting opinions in regard to a second operation on my neck. That had confused and upset both me and my family.

Dr. Flanagan and I have often discussed ways to improve communication between Ralph and me, which has been an ongoing problem for me. One time he said, "Try to encourage him to express how he feels. Get him to air his views."

I sighed. "That's a great idea, but when I try to discuss things with him he often does not respond at all. I wind up giving a monologue."

"It might help if you ask him to make you aware that he heard what you have said."

"Sometimes when I have asked he repeated my words, yet he had made no response. But I hear you. I'll keep trying."

Because of other suggestions he offered, I now try to give more reassurance while discussing problems with Ralph and talk them over during a calm, pleasant time. We have talked about the importance of maintaining a partnership that gives us the right and responsibility to comment and make suggestions, without expecting perfection.

Something Dr. Flanagan told me that I particularly liked was, when appropriate, to say, "I need to have you be sensitive to, and respect, my sensitivity. I also need to have you think well of me."

I have kept the questions I had for him and the notes from some of our appointments in a special notepad. It's a good thing because, as important as his comments have been to me, some have been forgotten just when I needed them most.

During one appointment I said, "It's discouraging. I can't reduce my weight no matter what I do. I know lithium is part of the problem, but I can't give that up."

"Lithium does not make you overweight. It changes your metabolism. That means that you need daily exercise."

"Don't get me wrong, I'm grateful for lithium. It ended the nightmare I was living. Guess I'll simply have to increase my exercise program. Obviously, twice a week is not working for me. Cutting down on what I put in my mouth hasn't worked either."

He undoubtedly had the right answer me, but I must confess that I have failed to follow that advice. Far too often I've been so involved in writing that exercises were completely forgotten, except for the two times a week. I'll have to find a way to give it more priority, like I do my lithium treatment.

One day after arguing with Ralph about some ridiculous thing, I was furious when he said, "You're so sensitive." I wished I could remember what to say when he attacked my sensitivity. I felt ashamed for letting things build up and irritate me. In spite of how much we love each other, silly arguments keep reoccurring.

There must be an answer.

After rereading my notes I vowed I'd try harder to avoid such foolish squabbles. Some day we would put an end to the unpleasant arguments and bickering that crept in unannounced. Maybe it would help to say, "Okay, honey," when the issue was trivial, and express how it made me feel if it seemed important.

I fantasized about it. I would ask Dr. Flanagan, "Remember how Ralph and I used to quarrel? Well, we've agreed to be more tolerant of each other's faults. We had a contest to see which one could say the most complimentary, yet sincere, things to each other." Then I would add, "It's been fun, and would you believe this? We ended in a tie."

Back to reality. I *have* to learn to risk expressing my anger as irritation occurs. I must not let it build up to an angry explosion, or into physical symptoms. That must be something else Dr. Flanagan told me, it sounds so wise.

In January, 1990 he was appointed Medical Director of Charter Hospital of San Diego, an excellent neuropsychiatric facility not too far from my home. This hospital treats mental illness and chemical dependency for both inpatients and outpatients. I am proud of him, as well as relieved to be able to continue as his patient. I was afraid he would be too busy to continue his private practice.

He and all his predecessors since 1973 have helped me understand my illness. In addition, they have greatly improved the quality of my life.

 *Notes:*

14

The Family

The greatest happiness of life is the conviction that we are loved ... for ourselves, or rather, loved in spite of ourselves
—Victor Hugo

Early symptoms of depression are easily overlooked by the family. None of us realized anything was wrong when I felt tired, yet hadn't done anything to tire myself, or ate less and lost weight without being on a diet. If we did notice, we quite naturally were not alarmed.

As the symptoms became more obvious and intense, our girls went through a period of shock and disbelief. They have told me they had conversations like the following:

"How could Mom change so much?"

"Yeah. She has always kept herself up."

"And she was outgoing and a lot of fun."

"But now, she's usually in her robe and just stands like a statue, or sits and stares."

"Not only that. If she says anything at all it's gloom and doom."

"I scarcely know her. It's awful."

"And I don't know what to say or do."

One of the things Ralph did for me was to take me out to dinner once a week. He had to select my clothes when I was depressed. If he had not, we would have arrived at the restaurant after closing time.

Typically, he would say, "How would you like to go out to dinner tonight? It would be a nice change for you."

"All right, but I don't know what to wear."

"Don't worry. I'll get something out for you."

After we were seated at the restaurant, he'd say, "What would you like for dinner?"

After reading and rereading the menu several times, I would tell him, "I just can't decide."

"Well, you like prime rib, why not have that?"

"Okay, that's fine."

"Want the salad?"

"I don't care."

"What kind of dressing?"

"You just order. Okay?"

Although going out gave us a change from our usual routine, I was anything but a scintillating companion.

I have often looked back and marveled at how Ralph handled all his extra responsibilities, yet continued to work while I was hospitalized. He had to pay the bills, be a good parent, and shop. He also had to do the laundry and prepare meals, assisted by our youngest daughter, Linda. In addition, he elected to visit me every day and twice a day on weekends. He did it all without complaint. If he had complained, I am sure I would have felt guiltier than ever, if that's possible.

After my discharge from the hospital, his duties eased up somewhat, but he still had to cope with my mood swings. Until a two-month cycle evolved, he didn't know which wife he'd come home to. Would it be the silent, lethargic, tousle-haired one who still wore a soiled housecoat and a vacant stare? Or would it be the gabby, tireless sexpot wearing a black lace nightie and a provocative smile?

* * *

It was not until years later that I fully realized what a challenge I must have been to my family during the vacillating mood swings.

It's a pity they were unaware that during each depressive phase I felt smothered under a heavy, oppressive blanket. I was unable to describe it, let alone throw it off. And no one else could do it for me. Knowing that, might have lightened their burden of guilt—a little.

Like other clinically depressed people, I was unable to absorb the hope my family offered. Negative thoughts and emotions far outweighed it. Undaunted, they continued to offer their encouragement.

Being invited to a daughter's or friend's home for dinner provided a welcome change during the black lows. As I look back a welcome alternative, at times, would have been having someone bring us an entree for dinner.

I often wished I could have help with the laundry. I agonized over how to pre-treat the spots, how much soap to use, and even about how long to set the timer. I was too ashamed to ask for help.

Fortunately, my loved ones treated me as a mature, normal adult throughout the years of mood swings, including my return home after the three hospitalizations. I was unaware of their ever being oversolicitous or overprotective. Instead, they remained as tactful, considerate, and affectionate as ever.

The manic episodes had the power to destroy relationships with both family and friends. Not everyone can tolerate them. Ralph pointed out realities when I insisted on doing something outrageous, like going into business. I resisted his efforts, or simply tuned out his remarks. When manic, I thought I knew and could do anything and everything. I felt omnipotent.

Coping with me was undoubtedly difficult for everyone. During manic phases I had no idea my behavior was inappropriate. With chagrin, I remember propositioning a friend of ours. Fortunately, he declined. That happened just before I left Ralph, in a manic fury. I did not realize that my inhibitions and judgment ranged from low to nil.

Luckily for me, my family accepted my ludicrous actions, forked tongue, and filibusters. We have always been closely knit.

Our mutual love, plus our friends' thoughtfulness, helped sustain us during those grueling years.

In addition to their emotional support, Ralph and the girls had the innate ability to know what to say or not say, although they didn't realize it. They did *not* make any unfeeling remarks such as: "Pull yourself together. Think positive." Or, "Don't be so darned negative."

Like other mental illnesses, this one challenged both my family and me, as I have indicated. It had the power to either drive a wedge between us or to bind us closer. How glad I was, and still am, that we became closer.

Many spouses and family members react badly when this disorder strikes. Some abandon the relationship. Others torment the patient with verbal abuse. They do not understand, or try to understand, what has happened, or why the patient will not simply do something about the situation. They ignorantly make assumptions, ignoring the fact that the person certainly would change if it were possible. Do they think anyone enjoys feeling and acting that way?

People such as I have described say things such as, "Why don't you snap out of it? You have everything to make you happy." Or, "Get your butt out of bed. How can you be so lazy?" Unfeeling comments like that could easily intensify the patient's delusions of being worthless. The person is *not* worthless, but is convinced that he or she is.

The family of a manic-depressive friend of mine turned on her, saying, "What's the matter with you? You must be crazy." Her torment became more excruciating than before. After that, the entire family, with the exception of one brother, had nothing to do with her. I don't know how she survived. I have been most fortunate.

Some relatives begin to hate the patient. They need to learn to love and accept the person, but there is nothing wrong with hating the symptoms.

No do-it-yourself kit will fix mental illness. I know from both experience and research that getting competent professional help is of prime importance.

Not everyone in the family will suffer from this disorder, but there can be a genetic predisposition or weakness. It is important to remember that predisposition does *not* mean predestined.

If anyone in our family had symptoms that persisted over two weeks and prevented ordinary functioning, I would insist on finding well-qualified professional help. If the person objected I would say, "Sorry, but you have no options. I have made an appointment with a physician that I know can help you."

It has been most gratifying to me to note the progress made in the mental health field. Today's patients and their families no longer have to function under additional handicaps of ignorance and discouragement. In addition, they no longer need to feel alone.

Support groups are available. At the (nationwide) Charter Hospital in our area, Ralph recently visited the group for families while I visited the one for patients. Both of us were impressed by the facility, and by the friendliness and sharing found in each group. The one I visited reminded me of Dr. Smith's group, except there were no hecklers there to make anyone squirm.

Today, when family members become aware of unusual, persistent changes in the moods and behavior of a loved one, information is there for the asking. Many articles and books are published about mental illnesses. (See Appendix A)

Another good source of information is government agencies. They promptly answer requests for their data. My files include data from D/ART, (Depression/Awareness/Recognition/Treatment) a division of the National Institute of Mental Health. Literature is available from both agencies, and others. (See Appendix A)

Ideally, all manic-depressives would receive an accurate diagnosis, treatment, and information from their physicians. If they or their families wanted more information they could buy books or borrow them at the library, or request information from government agencies such as those mentioned. Everyone who is so inclined can easily become informed about this disorder. Enlightenment is at their fingertips. Our family was unaware of this when my mood swings affected us all so deeply.

 *Notes:*

15

Family Feelings

The weight of this sad time we must obey, speak what we feel; not what we ought to say.—Shakespeare

No one knew how to help me while I floundered through the acute phase of my illness. Our family and friends were completely baffled by the symptoms. Each depressive episode affected everyone involved. Gloom permeated the atmosphere. No one could cheer me up. Our entire family, like many others, continued to share in my suffering as the illness persisted. They gave so much, and received so little.

With no diagnosis, information, or encouragement from the psychoanalyst, our struggle was compounded. We were in desperate need of supportive help with our fears, guilt, and other problems.

After many years, both Cathi and Linda told me, "I tortured myself with questions like, 'What did I do wrong? How could this ever happen to Mom?'"

Ralph said, "I kept wondering whether I had done anything that could have made you sick."

Janie told me, "I felt guilty for years about my doctor referring you to Dr. Jones and the first hospital, especially when both did you more harm than good."

Cathi said, "I wish I'd never taken you to that so-called 'healer' when you first got sick."

It's pitiful that they did not realize that they were not the cause of any of my misery. Both my positive and rational thoughts were off on a trip during the years of the mood swings. Constructive thinking could not return until the chemical imbalance was dealt with and controlled. Our three daughters, in many ways, reacted differently to those traumatic years. Some of their recollections are different from mine, but I have not changed them. Their words are exactly as they recalled our experiences.

Linda was so disturbed that she ran away from the memories. When she could admit that to me, I urged her to get them down on paper, which she did. Her notes enlarged upon some things I knew, but revealed other things I did not know until she let me read what she had written:

> I remember the terrible time you had deciding what to wear. You stood in front of your closet with an agonized look on your face, strenuously wringing your hands, as if you were hurting yourself. You did that whenever you had to make any decision. It seemed unreal to me that you could be immobilized by depression.
>
> The evening of the suicide attempt, after being unable to find a hospital where you could be admitted, Dad brought you home. I realized more fully than ever before how deeply he loved you. He held me in his arms and cried, while asking me how he could help *me*. I was amazed that he could do that when his own pain was so intense.
>
> The same evening, I remember reading the Sunday funnies to you. I had hoped to brighten you up a little, but you didn't respond at all. After while I went into my room, shut the door, and cried. I remembered that Cathi had cautioned, "Don't look in the washer."

Then she reluctantly explained, "That's where I put the rugs from Mom's bathroom."

When I saw you, I told myself those gauze-wrapped wrists must belong to a stranger, not to my Mom.

As time went by, the loss of feeling in your fingers persisted, due to nerve damage, the surgeon told you. You hated the constant reminder of what you had done. You were furious with yourself. Sometimes you gritted your teeth and shook your head and your body in frustration. You shook your fist at the floor.

Years later, I hated the shock treatments you had. To me, they represented a frightening unknown. So much stigma had been attached to them. And afterwards, you didn't remember some things. That scared me, because I had no idea it would just be temporary. I wanted desperately to understand. I kept asking myself, how could Mom feel that way? I felt so closely identified with my parents and siblings I tried to drive myself into despair deep enough to make me understand. I even thought about suicide, so I could experience your pain.

Cathi had a crisis and wound up in Cedars Sinai Hospital, where she had both private and group therapy. I saw her doctor only once, as I recall, and told him, "I'm terrified. If it could happen to Mom, it could happen to me." Especially since Cathi broke down and wound up on a psychiatric ward.

In time, I came to realize that each one of us is a separate entity. I did not have to create my mother's experience in my own life.

We stood in her kitchen as we discussed her notes. Linda said, "I didn't know what a catharsis it could be to write all that stuff down. At times, after you started writing your book, you asked me whether I could tell you how I felt about your illness. I couldn't express it verbally, but I'm so relieved that I could write it out."

Regrettably, she had buried some of those intense feelings for twenty-four years. She came to realize that was not a wise thing to do. She became aware of how important it is for people to get professional help when their problems seem insurmountable.

"Those feelings I had," she added, "bobbed up out of the subconscious briefly at times, but they really surfaced when I edited your book."

"I'm glad they finally did, honey, but so sorry it had to take so long."

"I feel as if I've been healed, Mom. This is wonderful." Linda and I hugged each other—a warm, heartfelt embrace.

Initially, Cathi was unable to write down her feelings about my illness, but we discussed them briefly, and I took notes. Later, I wrote them out to clarify them and put them in the mail, as requested. She then expounded on her feelings and, as she put it, "edited the editor." She added, "Once I got started, I didn't know how to stop."

This is what she had to say:

> When you were so sick, we all helped each other to help you, but none of us could confide our fears and feelings about ourselves. We *never* expressed the effect the illness was having on *us*. We now find out that each one of us felt guilty about your illness, and extremely angry and hurt about many things. It took your writing this book for the three of us to finally talk about it.
>
> While I was growing up, I had always been told by your friends and/or acquaintances that I was just like you. When you fell apart, I was afraid that if I was just like you, then I'd fall apart too. Plus, I found out you weren't perfect. What a shock that was! When I started having seizures, and ended up on a psych ward, I certainly felt those fears were valid.

* * *

And then, years later, you warned all of us that
your illness was hereditary and that we should be
aware of and not neglect symptoms. This increased
my fears for a while, until I became much more
secure within myself. You even told my [teenage]
son about the hereditary aspect of the illness, and my
hospitalization. This has caused him to occasionally
be afraid if I become even a little bit irrational.

The infliction of this fear in him has awakened
some of my fears and anger. I don't think he needed
to be "warned" or that he had any need to know about
my hospitalization. At times it has undermined my
control/authority over him; at others, just created
fears for him. I truly feel that grandchildren, as
children, don't have a "need to know." Once they are
adults, then if the occasion arises to discuss the
illness, there's no need to try to hide it. But why
inflict all the fears and anxieties on a child over
something that occurred 25 years ago? I don't want
him to have to live through what we did—watching
and waiting.

Mom, there were so many times before you got
better when you would level out for a little while and
we would think you were "cured." Then when you
started into one of your depressive swings, we would
become so afraid. Most of us could deal fairly well
with the manic ones, (except Dad, because they were
so costly) but the depressive stage was the most
devastating of all.

Sometimes you wouldn't speak for days and
unless we physically took you by the hand and
moved you, you would stay in exactly the same spot
you had drifted to or last been taken. I can remember
even having to take you to and from the toilet because
we were afraid you wouldn't remember to go. You
told me once that during the depressive stages the old

nursery rhyme, "The worms go in, the worms go out, the worms play pinochle on my snout ...." continually went 'round and 'round in your head. That must have been ghastly for you. It still hurts me so to know you were hurting that much.

And I'll never be able to forget walking into, and later cleaning, the bathroom where you had attempted suicide. I had rushed to your home when I heard about the attempt, and was trying desperately to get everything cleaned up before Linda got home from school. I called her school and made them promise me that they would keep her there, no matter how long it took, until I could pick her up. And now, after reading Linda's excerpt, I find I still scared her anyway, by warning her not to open the washer, where I was soaking the carpets and towels.

Now, as an adult, I wonder why in the world I was trying so hard to get the stains out, instead of throwing everything away. I think of all the years of your ups and downs, those few days were the most devastating and caused most of the anxiety we felt whenever you became depressed afterwards.

Something else that terrified me was your loss of memory. I remember, even before we knew of your illness, we would leave you notes; you would read them and throw them away, and then forget you had ever read them.

But it really hurts when we talk with you about things that were hard for us, and you don't remember them at all.

We all learned to live our lives with our grief and sorrow. I'm sorry, Mom, but I just couldn't read your manuscript. I started to, but it stirred everything up—the desolation, anger and fears. I couldn't sleep for two nights. I have to let it all go.

But on the good side, I know the experiences of your illness contributed to my being who I am.

After reading what Cathi had written, I called to apologize for unknowingly upsetting her and our grandson, and to say, "I'm glad *something* good came from that stressful time."

"It did, Mom, so please don't worry about it. We love you, and are really proud of you for writing your story."

She told me she was relieved to get it out. Again she said that once she got started she had no difficulty, but after finishing she wanted to let it all go.

Janie's recollections were from an autobiography she had written a few years ago. This is what was valid to her:

> Mom went to a counseling center in the mid-1960's to get help. I believe that, instead of helping her to deal with deep feelings of shame, guilt, and low self-esteem, they pumped her up. They told her how great she is, how wonderful she is with people, both of which are true, and made her a lay counselor—until her bubble burst. She finally became overwhelmed with her responsibilities—perhaps wondering how she could help others when she so desperately needed help herself—and she withdrew; she began acting like a little child, a small infant who could not verbalize or do anything for herself.
>
> I first learned of this bizarre behavior when my sister, Cathi, and (half) sister, Linda, called me at Rocketdyne for help. Our (step) dad, Ralph, was away at Army Reserve Summer Camp. The people at the counseling center were making arrangements for a woman to come and stay with Mom during the day, while my sisters were at school. They advised us not to leave Mom alone for any period of time whatsoever. I took off like a shot from work—after calling my husband, Bob, to let him and our four children know what was going on—and went to Mom's home in Palos Verdes.
>
> Somehow, within the next few days, and I hon-

estly don't remember how, I managed to locate Ralph and have the Army fly him back home to be with us through this family crisis. Mom was not speaking to us. We had to bathe her, dress her, feed her, take her to the bathroom, and put her to bed. I warned Ralph to stay with her until the homecare lady arrived and went back to the San Fernardo Valley to take care of my own family and return to work.

Ralph apparently didn't comprehend the seriousness of Mom's situation. About 30 minutes before the counseling lady was due to arrive, he apparently decided that as long as he was home, he might as well go back to work ... after all, what can happen in 30 minutes?

Well, when the lady got there, she found Mom in the master bathroom, bleeding and unconscious, with both of her wrists slashed.

What a nightmare!

I felt so bad!

Ralph had warned me once, when I was very young, "Never, ever trust anyone. Not even me!" And he was right. I should have stayed and found her competent medical help. Because of Bob's [her husband] connections with the Health Department, I got stuck with the task, anyway, of trying to find a good psychiatrist that would treat her both in a hospital setting and outside the hospital—when she was well enough to come home. I finally found one with a private practice, who also worked in a psychiatric hospital in the area.

Mom was released, still childlike, from the regular hospital after she recovered from surgery to tie the nerve endings of her wrists back together. I took additional unpaid time off from work to go with Mom and Ralph to commit her to the psychiatric facility. Ralph, predictably, said, "Since you're here, Janie, there's no point in my hanging around—I'll go back to work." He signed what he was required to sign and left me there to help Mom through the admissions procedure!

She was still not talking, although you could tell by her eyes that she had some awareness of what was going on. When it came time for her to sign the insurance papers, she refused. As many times as I put the pen into her hand and said, "Mom, please sign the forms so they can start your treatment," she just opened her hand and let the pen fall out.

She told me later that the reason she didn't want to sign was, "I wanted Ralph to have to pay for all of the expenses himself." She and he had argued about money for years, and she didn't want the insurance company to pay for anything!

Mom was finally diagnosed a "bipolar manic-depressive" with a "chemical imbalance"—after enduring several episodes of severe depression, undergoing electrical shock treatments, and spending time in a couple of psychiatric hospitals where she finally learned (I hope) to love herself and to express her artistic talents.

How did all of this make me feel? It scared me! It also made me feel guilty. What more could I have done to prevent this from happening? Had I failed her as a daughter and friend? How did I let her down? And it made me very, very angry with my step-father. Dammit, he should have stayed home with my mother and should never have left me alone in the hospital with her! She's my Mom! She's sick! This is more than I can bear alone!

How did I really feel? I didn't. I couldn't. If I had allowed myself to feel, I would have been hysterical. I would have fallen to pieces. I had to remain strong for the sake of my mother, my sisters, and my own four children. In a way, perhaps I did fall to pieces—or at least split off. I couldn't feel. The real me couldn't bear the pain, so the calm, cool, collected me took over.

Several years later, my own depression, after my second husband left me, also frightened me. I slept for a week with a rifle cradled in my arms, trying to get up enough nerve to blow my brains out. I wasn't going to take any chances on botching the job like Mom had. The only thing that stopped me was the thought of what it would do to my children. And then I realized that it was time for me to stop living to meet the needs of others and start living to meet my own needs.

I was terribly afraid of being manic-depressive, too, but I found a wonderful psychiatrist in Van Nuys, Michael Coburn, who saw me through this time. Mike helped me to understand that anyone going through what I was going through, and had been through, would naturally be depressed given the same circumstances. What I was experiencing was a perfectly normal reaction! I just needed to pick up the pieces and get on with my life. And pick up the pieces, I did! So, thank God, have Mom and Ralph and my sisters.

Mom's in her seventies now, takes lithium carbonate daily, like a diabetic has to take insulin, and is living a full and productive life. She's very creative, writes beautiful Christmas poems, has a computer, and is working on a novel. And she paints so well that her art has been shown and sold to others—who appreciate the depth and quality of her work. She and Ralph recently celebrated their fortieth wedding anniversary. Our family is very close.

We all really love Mom and are proud of her for overcoming this potentially tragic disease—and of Ralph for growing with her and deepening their relationship. All of us work together to show her how much we truly love her and try to protect her from stressful situations.

* * *

Ralph was finally able to write down what he recalls about my illness. He titled it HUSBAND'S MEMORIES:

After twenty-five years of living with a person who has bipolar illness, I will attempt to reveal my side of the illness, as I recall being exposed to it when it occured.

Initially, I was very shocked and bewildered when notified that I should return home from Summer Camp as soon as possible, due to my spouse's illness. I could not understand her actions, nor could I find any reason for them. Not having previous experience along this line, nor any knowledge of anyone who had had this illness, I was at a loss as to what to do.

I knew that she had studied counseling and had been working at the Counseling Service, but she did not bring other people's problems home with her for discussion. She has always tried to help other people with their problems.

When I got home, I didn't realize the extent of her depression. After her suicide attempt, I tried to get her into a hospital for care. We went to the Los Angeles County General Hospital seeking admission or help, only to be referred to private hospitals. I found out that in order to be admitted for treatment, it was necessary for her to be admitted by a doctor on the staff of that hospital. We finally found one not too far from home, with a doctor on their staff that could admit her. My action was to have her get treatment to cure the illness as soon as possible and return her to a normal life.

After about six weeks in the hospital, she was released as an outpatient. I dropped her off at the hospital in the morning, on my way to work, and would pick her up in the evening, on my way home. (Come to think of it, I think that was after her second hospitalization.)

After her release from the hospital she saw the doctor, a psychoanalyst, twice a week. After about five years the doctor told me that he had to see her three times a week, in order to follow her case close enough. I told him, "We have to eat too," as I was convinced that he was not doing anything for her. At about that time, a friend of hers suggested that she see the doctor that she was going to. She had discussed Charlotte's case with him. I talked it over with my wife. We agreed, as she too was ready for a change of doctors.

The new doctor immediately told her that she had a chemical imbalance in her brain, and promptly set about to correct it. He also told us that it wasn't necessary to see her three times a week. He wanted to see her twice a week to start, but to quickly cut her visits to once a week, then once in two weeks, and eventually to four times a year (only because he was prescribing medicine for her, and needed to check up on it).

This doctor was interested in curing her, and not interested in our supporting him.

She is still taking lithium carbonate, and is under psychiatric care, but is only seen four times a year. Her lithium level is monitored quarterly, and the lithium intake is adjusted when necessary.

She has had to change doctors several times, due to their demise or retirement, or our moving, but she has always been able to find doctors that are interested in keeping her well. Whenever it is necessary to find another doctor, she first makes sure that he believes in and uses lithium treatment.

I have always tried to give my spouse *love, comfort, support and understanding.* That's what I think she needs and wants the most.

* * *

It has grieved me, and still does, that Ralph, our daughters, and grandson have had to endure so much pain and suffering because of my illness. We have our own unique viewpoints about the experience. There is no doubt about the powerful impact it has had on each one of us. Fortunately, we have all grown considerably as a result.

With all the progress made in regard to diagnosis, medication, and treatment, and the information available today, surely people's fears will be overcome. It is radically different today than when I suffered from bipolar disorder and had those acute years of inadequate treatment.

I am trying, currently, to convince our daughters that they do not have to protect me from stress. Effective treatment of my disease, including psychotherapy, has made me a stronger person than ever before. I do not want to be shielded. Stressful events, which are bound to happen in any family, are things I have found I can take in stride.

A friend once told me, and I cherish the thought, "Out of the mud, the lotus grows."

 *Notes:*

16

Stigma and Progress

The great obstacle to progress is prejudice.—Bovee

For centuries, stigma has added its burden to the mentally ill and to their families. Its strong footing has caused a culture lag.

Beams of light have begun to pierce the darkness of misconception. Groups, as well as individuals, have been striving to overcome this situation. An estimated fifteen percent of the U. S. population suffer from some form of diagnosable mental illness. It can happen to anyone.

Modern research has shown that many groups of behavioral syndromes are caused by a treatable brain disease. It is a no-fault brain disease, yet the victims are still called "crazy," "bonkers," "maniacs," and more. It makes me shudder when I read or hear such inconsiderate terms. Yet I understand that comments like that are a result of prejudice and lack of accurate information. Sometimes such labels are used as a defense mechanism by family members, who fear that they are responsible for their relative's symptoms.

Why must a psychiatric hospital be called a "loony bin," a "funny farm," or a "booby hatch?" That still happens, in spite of the progress that has been made in the mental health field. I believe the term "snake pit" has finally become obsolete; I hope the other offensive labels will soon be replaced. Education is gradually reducing stigma just as it has been reduced for diabetes, epilepsy, and other medical conditions.

Understandably, as a person who has a major mental disorder, I am biased against that degrading terminology. Mood disorders such as mine are still regarded by uninformed and insensitive people as character weaknesses. That and other distorted views have done nothing but add to the pain of those who are already suffering from the illness.

Why should anyone with what is now known to be a biological disorder be taunted, treated with condescension, or worse, be subjected to discrimination? As the facts become more widely known, surely the stigma will be overcome.

I have escaped most of those ordeals, but have experienced the misplaced concern of a few individuals who asked during a minor stressful time, "Are you *sure* you're all right?" That happened after I had been without mood swings for years.

"Yes, don't worry about me. I'm fine," I said.

They usually cocked their heads to one side and patted my shoulder while they asked. I wondered whether they thought the slightest stress might send me into orbit. Did they think they had to walk on eggs when around me? Little did they know that when the illness was controlled the eggs were made of stainless steel!

Years before those incidents, I had a most uncomfortable encounter with stigma. It happened prior to my receiving lithium treatment, while easing out of a depressive episode and into a manic one. I began to fill out a lengthy job application. It included questions about previous positions, when and what I did while employed, *and* what I did when unemployed. They also asked specifics about hospitalizations.

My feeling of confidence when I walked into that place of

business quickly disappeared. Should I reveal that a severe depression had led to a suicide attempt and hospitalization in a psychiatric unit? I started to tremble, and had to get out of there fast. I was afraid to reveal the truth—and unable to lie.

Several years after my mood swings were under control, I felt uncomfortable about telling my bridge club I could no longer attend. The reason was that my therapy group had begun to meet the same day. I gave some other excuse.

The tug of war between stigma and need for approval and acceptance kept me from revealing the real reason. It took me a long time to come up with that insight. Group therapy later helped me accept myself and my illness more fully. I became able to admit, whenever appropriate, that I was manic-depressive.

Now I realize that to tell someone I am manic-depressive means being responsible for providing that person with brief, accurate, credible information about the disorder.

At one time I wondered whether my primary care doctor was under the influence of stigma. Had he thought the ailment he was treating had not responded to treatment because of my history of mental illness?

When an upper respiratory infection and bronchitis did not respond to treatment, he recommended several vitamins, minerals, herb tea, and more. Perhaps I overreacted. I found another doctor.

Not too long ago I filled out a form at a dentist's office. It asked whether I had ever had a nervous disorder. I wrote, "manic-depression," although unsure at the time whether it fit into that category. It did. Did they think I would be a more difficult patient? Or what?

Why hadn't they also asked whether the disorder was under control? If they had, I could have said yes.

An appalling example of stigma used as a weapon was the negative campaign that knocked Senator Eggleston out of a vice-presidential race. Following the death of his brother, he had a depression that required treatment. I admired him for getting help. I hoped the day would soon come when that type of prejudice would be eliminated from the political scene.

In the January 6, 1992 issue of *Time Magazine's* Man of the

Year, Ted Turner, of CNN, identified himself as a successfully treated manic-depressive. As mental disorders become better understood, an enlightened attitude could lessen the massive and prolonged stigma. The situation has clamored to be changed.

Only one in three victims of mood disorders seeks treatment. Appalling, isn't it? What makes it even more appalling is that it is largely because of both shame and stigma. Other causes are lack of awareness of the symptoms and the difference between "the blues" and clinical depression.

On the positive side, of the people who do get help for mood disorder, 80 - 90 percent have significant symptom relief. Despair can be lessened for the victims of this illness as people become more aware of the facts about the affliction.

Many sources agree that the stigma that permeates depressive illnesses is caused by fear of the unknown in both ourselves and in others. Ignorance and prejudice also provide a breeding ground for stigma. These straight jackets of misconception have begun to be removed as more information has become available. NIMH (National Institute of Mental Health) states, "90 percent of what we know about the brain we have learned in the last ten years." To overcome their fears, the public needs to get the facts.

Get the facts and fear no more!

Even in the medical community, some individuals see mental illness as a disgrace, as in the case of a friend of mine who had a depressive episode and was fired while working as a psychiatric nurse!

In spite of all the delays, I have a strong feeling that, through education, the long, dark history of stigma will eventually be overcome. Many steps of progress have been taken in mental health. Predictably, giant strides will be made in the years ahead. As a result, stigma will become as obsolete as the covered wagon.

 *Notes:*

17

Moods, Creativity, and Fame

The way to fame is like the way to heaven, through much tribulation.—Sterne

A surprising number of famous people have been tormented by depressive illnesses, some in the past, others in the present. They achieved fame in spite of their affliction. Creativity appeared to be the golden thread that tied them together.

According to Reader's Digest's *ABC's of the Human Mind*, "Creativity seems entwined with mental illness, particularly the bipolar sort characterized by agonizing swings between deep, spiritless depression and boundless, enthusiastic energy."

Joshua Logan, who was manic-depressive, candidly discussed his illness in his book, *Josh*. Like me, he lost his father when he was little. I lost mine when I was seven months old. We both spent many years seeking substitutes.

Logan was a producer-director whose hits included "South Pacific," "Picnic," and "Mister Roberts." My "hits" were Janie, Cathi, and Linda.

Patty Duke struggled through untreated manic-depression

from its onset in 1970 until her illness was diagnosed in 1982. That was when she began lithium treatment. She won an Oscar for her starring role in "Miracle Worker." She has also starred in many other outstanding movies. Her autobiography, "Call Me Anna," co-authored with Kenneth Turan, revealed her poignant reactions to this complex disease. She has continued to do all she can to bring about understanding and acceptance of the illness.

Vivien Leigh, particularly reknown for her tempestuous role as Scarlett in "Gone With the Wind," also suffered from depressive disorders. So did Lincoln, Edison, Churchill, and Hemingway.

A recent study linked creative genius and emotional problems. I was fascinated to learn that mood disorders had a positive aspect. Creative manic-depressives include: Poe, Byron, Shelley, Tennyson, Rossetti, Eugene O'Neill, Virginia Woolf, and F. Scott Fitzgerald.

Since 1985, special concerts called "Moods and Music" have been given in San Diego as part of an effort to challenge the stigma of mental illness. The aim was to increase understanding and acceptance of both depressive and manic-depressive disorders, and to encourage individuals to seek treatment.

Comprehensive information in the front part of the 1989 program, written by Dr. Kay Redfield Jamison, should have gone a long way toward accomplishing that goal. That particular concert featured the music of five gifted composers who were manic-depressive: Handel, Schumann, Wolf, Mahler, and Berlioz. Sponsors of the events were all prominent in the field of mental health.

I felt excited and gratified to discover that such efforts were being made. More was being done to improve the field of mental health than I had realized or even dreamed.

After my mood swings were controlled, I began to enjoy my own creative efforts, but with no delusions about being a genius. It became important to express myself in creative ways. Painting was my prime interest for ten years.

My oil painting lessons began and ended temporarily during the active phase of my illness. After the moods were under control, I resumed the classes. I sold many of my paintings, and even did several commissions. Our daughters selected their favorites, which added to my joy.

Writing came later; it continues to be a strong, magnetic force in my life. Both creative outlets have brought immense satisfaction.

All of my creative outlets have been therapeutic. They required concentration. While completely absorbed in creating something there is no time to think or worry about anything else.

Those endeavors have added an extra dimension to my life. Learning how to do new things caused me to look at the world in a different light and to see things that had gone unnoticed before.

As an artist I saw colors, forms, shadows, and textures more vividly. As a writer I became more tuned in on people, conversations, and facial expressions. Ideas for writing began to bombard me from every direction.

Creative expression has added to my self-confidence and increased my feelings of self-worth, based on achievement. Self-worth, on a deeper level, has evolved from striving to develop spiritually. I learned to place more value on myself, as a person unified with a Supreme Being, rather than basing it on how well I accomplished things. I acquired beliefs that helped sustain me when life was particularly challenging.

The accomplishments of the famous people I've mentioned, and others like them, have been an inspiration. They have demonstrated that mood disorders do not have to hold us back, but can urge us on to greater heights.

Notes:

18

Growth, Research, and Hope

Hope ... like the sun, casts the shadow of our burden behind us.—S. Smiles

During a vacation trip through the state of Washington, I was amazed to see new growth surging out of charred, cut, and broken snags of trees that appeared to be dead. Puzzled, I discovered that the damaged "nurser" trees nourished the new growth. The young saplings were more flexible, yet stronger and more resplendent than the original trees.

I resolved that my illness would be the "nurser" for my own growth. That is when I began to learn how to do the creative things that had intrigued me for years. To paraphrase Shakespeare, my desolation began to make a better life for me. Before that turning point I had not taken the time.

My new-found activities brought immense satisfaction, but I think the best outgrowth from my illness has come from increased empathy and compassion. I concluded that our own suffering enables us to see the world in many different perspectives and to be more sensitive. Pain seems more painful and pleasure more pleasurable. I agree with Dr. Jamison who said that mental illness does not have to be a total disaster.

One of my greatest rewards has come from answering cries for help from friends who were close to an undiagnosed person with symptoms of manic-depression. In one instance the doctor had prescribed megavitamins for a friend's daughter, who became worse instead of better. Alarmed, the mother called me seeking advice. She had seen me before and after I received lithium treatment.

I explained to her that people with manic-depressive symptoms needed to be aware that different treatments are suggested, but responses vary according to the individual. Since her daughter did not respond well to one form of treatment and the mother was so unhappy with the doctor, I asked, "Why don't you look for another professional opinion? When I changed doctors the seesaw course of the illness ended."

Quite naturally I thought she would be equally lucky. I recommended my own psychiatric physician, confident that he could resolve her problem. She said, "I don't see how I can go that far. I will have to find someone closer to home."

Among other things, I told her that D/ART had excellent literature available about the disorder. She assured me that she would request some and find another doctor.

Another friend wanted to know whether stress brought on the illness. Dr. Brown's explanation had convinced me that other more important factors contribute to it. Stress could trigger an episode, but although related to mood disorders, not everyone with stress becomes depressed. Some individuals may develop symptoms with no apparent cause, including stress.

I had three major surgeries during the twelve months before the onset of my illness. They did not cause it. For several years before that I was upset by the traumatic marriage of our eldest daughter and the illness of another daughter. Those things did not cause it.

When I finally received a diagnosis, my new psychiatric physician told me what did. Dr. Brown said, "You have a genetic pre-disposition to manic-depression and a chemical imbalance of the brain. They caused your illness." The mystery was solved.

Many families are concerned about the genetic factor in this disease. Our daughters have been terrified that they would develop the symptoms.

Paraphrasing Dr. Mark S. Gold's book, *The Good News About Depression*, some studies have shown that if one parent and one child have a mood disorder, a sibling has a 25 percent risk of developing it. If both parents and one child have it the risk rises to 40 percent.

Depressive illness can skip generations as well as vary in both type and severity. While acute symptoms of manic-depression are present, the chaos and intensity of both moods and behavior can range from mild to debilitating, and the cycles from slow to rapid. Other patients' patterns could be quite different from mine.

One of our daughters became concerned about one of her children. She asked for information about my illness. After answering some of her questions, I told her that specialists recommend that family members with unexplained, prolonged psychological symptoms should go to a well-qualified professional to get an accurate evaluation.

Unlike manic-depression, temporary upsets can be triggered by traumatic events, such as the death of a loved one, divorce, job loss, rape, or moving to another community. Any of those could cause reactive depression, a normal response to traumatic upsets. In that type of depression there are many ways a person can cope, but in some cases professional help is necessary. It is different from manic-depression, which may be more severe, recurrent, and longer lasting.

Names for manic-depression that are used more currently include: bipolar illness, bipolar disorder, bipolar manic, bipolar mixed type, bipolar depression, or bipolar affective disorder. I used the term manic-depression because I thought it was more familiar to most people. Bipolar means the moods swing between two poles or extremes. As I have demonstrated, this serious affliction in its most extreme form plunges its victims from frenzied excitement to black, crushing despair. It can happen in a matter of hours, days, weeks, months, or years.

One day it struck me that the acronym for bipolar affective

disorder was BAD. That tickled my funnybone. It certainly was an apt way to describe it, so were the definitions offered in my dictionary. "Bad" was defined as: not acceptable, disagreeable, and unhappy state. Those words are certainly appropriate for both the illness and the patients' feelings about it.

Drs. Donald F. Klein and Paul H. Wender wrote a book called *Do You Have a Depressive Illness?* In it they said, "Depression and manic-depression are among the most common biological disorders seen in psychiatry. One woman in five and one man in ten can expect to develop a depression or manic-depression some-time in the course of their lives. In 1988 that would have meant well over 30 million people could have had the illness. Those are startling figures. And to think that in 1967 I thought I was the only one! The encouraging part is that of those who *do* seek help, 80 to 90 percent will have marked improvement.

Professionals who provide the essential care needed can be found in many places. It is available from psychiatrists, clinical psychologists, hospital departments of psychiatry, outpatient psychiatric clinics, family service/social agencies, community health centers, and private clinics and facilities. Hot lines are also available, including suicide prevention. They can be found in most telephone directories. In ours, they are in the front of the book. Personal recommendations can be particularly helpful.

Both patients and families should be aware that during a morbid depression suicide is a definite risk. Finding competent assistance can be a matter of life or death. 80 percent of all suicides occur because of depression.

My own desperate suicide attempt, near the onset of the disorder, clobbered me with merciless guilt and shame. It left noticeable scars on my wrists and numbness in my left hand. I became one of the world's worst typists, and still drop almost everything held in that hand.

Years later, the guilt was overcome. Well, almost overcome, but the physical reminders have been unremitting. They are relentless in their message that suicide is NOT the answer to desolation.

If only more despondent people could, and would, get professional help before desperation takes over. Their reasoning becomes biased by the distorted thinking associated with depression. Evidence of this is: hopelessness, helplessness, and the devastating misconception that "My family would be better off if I were dead!"

"Remember," Kent Layton remarked, "98 percent of the people who wish they were dead make a serious suicide attempt. One month later they are glad they are still alive." He should know. He is a director at Charter Hospital of San Diego.

Far too many diagnoses of depression are inaccurately based on physical illnesses. Dr. Gold pointed out, "At least 75 illnesses or conditions can cause symptoms of apparent mental disorder; some estimates are as high as 91. I call these diseases the Great Mimickers of psychiatry, for they imitate the disorders that psychiatrists are trained to treat."

Alcoholism is one of these. The underlying problem often goes undiagnosed because of the similarity of symptoms. The problem is compounded because many individuals, when they feel depressed and anxious have a "couple of drinks" to make them feel better. When they feel hyper, they have a "couple of drinks" to calm them down. Remember, drugs and alcohol make a mood disorder worse!

Symptoms may be caused by a side effect of illegal drugs. And many patients have been treated for schizophrenia, when they actually suffered from bipolar disorder. Accurate diagnosis of this disease is undoubtedly of prime importance in its effective treatment.

"Diagnostic tests for depression," according to Dr. Gold, "are designed to help the psychiatric physician render a specific diagnosis that pinpoints a specific treatment."

Symptoms alone are not an accurate way to make a diagnosis. As many as one-third of the misdiagnosed patients have what he calls an endocrine "mimicker." Of those, an underactive thyroid is the most frequent.

While under Dr. Brown's care, I was embarrassed to catch myself nodding off briefly while playing cards with Ralph. That was completely out of character for me. I also noticed an increasing lack of energy. Maybe I've been overdoing, I thought.

Then I woke up in the middle of the night shivering with cold. I piled on blankets, one after another, on my side of the bed. The next time I looked at the clock I discovered I had slept for ten hours. It startled me, since I had averaged seven to eight hours for years, except during the mood swings.

Still cold, I dressed in the warmest clothes I could find. That seemed strange too, since I often had to mop my brow while my friends were dressed comfortably in their sweaters. When I sat down to read the paper I found that I could scarcely hold it up. To remedy that situation I moved to Ralph's armchair so I could prop up both of my arms.

That did it. I called Dr. Brown. He had me come right in. It was a hot summer day, but I wore a heavy coat. As soon as he saw me he chuckled and said, "I know what your problem is, but we will check it out."

"What's wrong?"

"You are hypothyroid."

"What does that mean?"

"It means your thyroid gland is underactive. It could be a side effect from the lithium."

"I'm glad you know what it is. Now, what can we do about it? I'm tired of being so tired." I giggled at myself.

"I want you to get a blood test at your doctor's office, so we can verify my opinion. Taking thyroid pills should put an end to the problem in a few weeks."

As predicted, it did take a few weeks, but I enjoyed wearing the warm clothes that usually cluttered up my closet.

I am still manic-depressive, and always will be, but that is not the worst thing that could have happened to me. It could have been worse if I had not changed doctors and received the psychiatric care that worked for me, or if we had not had the insurance that helped provide that care.

It could have been worse if my illness had begun decades before 1971, the year that lithium was approved by the FDA, although I did not receive it until 1973.

It could have been far worse if my family had not been completely supportive.

And it could have been irrevocably worse if I had succeeded in the suicide attempt. I was truly blessed.

Considerable progress has been made in the mental health field in both diagnosis and treatment. As Dr. Gold remarked, tests can rule out organic causes. Aided by other clinical information, doctors can diagnose more accurately. His book revealed that other tests for depression point out the specific treatment that can free patients from being hopelessly mute and unresponsive. Improvement in many areas provides hope for the people who have felt devastated by their illness.

Currently, more is known about depression than any other psychological affliction. Tests have been developed that not only diagnose, but monitor and predict its course. When medication is required, tests can identify the correct dosage.

There is every reason for people who are afraid of getting a depressive illness, as well as those who have been devastated by it, to have hope. I like Dr. Gold's reassuring words, "For those who suffer mental agonies—the age of optimism has just begun."

For me it began in 1973, when Dr. Brown and lithium treatment brought my mood disorder under control. Although I have to rely indefinitely on medication and periodic monitoring, that has been no problem for me. I have been able to both enjoy and fully participate in life, without taking those pleasures for granted.

Highly skilled diagnosticians are now available: bio-psychiatrists, who specialize in diagnosis and appropriate treatment, psychiatric pharmocologists, and good psychiatrists well-trained in up-to-date biological psychiatry. Those who are board certified are also well qualified. Dr. Flanagan, my physician, fits into the latter category. All of these specialists are the most likely to give an accurate diagnosis. But no matter which expert is selected, it is important for the patient to feel comfortable with the physician.

After receiving treatment that was appropriate for me, my life was renewed. I have come a long way from thinking I was a failure at everything—including my getting better. It is hard to believe I ever felt that way.

I regained my sense of joy about each day, with all its pleasures and despite its problems, large and small. I moved on

from the bitter to the sweetness of life, which I became free to enjoy, without mood swings. I cherish it now more than ever.

It is my prayer that other people with mood disorders will receive the help they need before desperation impairs their reasoning. With effective treatment strength can evolve from agony. This is definitely a time of hope for those who are in the chasm of despair.

To anyone who has bipolar disorder, or any other depressive disorder, I want to repeat Dr. Smith's reassuring words, "Although manic-depression is an incurable mental illness, it is the *most treatable* one."

Remember, as Kent Layton said, "Don't hate the person with manic-depression; hate the symptoms. Be supportive to the person. Give empathy, not sympathy."

Remember too, "Hope ... like the sun, casts the shadow of our burden behind us."

AFTERWORD

This book would not be complete without my telling you that my problems with my mother were resolved a few years before her death. Before that, *most* of our time together was good. I only mentioned the incidents that caused me pain

Ralph didn't object to my writing about our difficulties, which I think is quite remarkable. As I became able to express both my positive and negative feelings more and more, our communication as well as our marital problems have inproved considerably. My physicians were right.

Our daughters have stopped trying to protect me. We express our feelings more openly. We don't believe in carrying grudges; we do believe in forgiveness. I'm glad.

Life is good.

APPENDIX A

WHERE TO FIND HELP

AMERICAN PSYCHIATRIC ASSOCIATION - for statistics, brochures/pamphlets, and to be on their mailing list. Can ask about research on your subject. Write or call: APA, Division of Public Affairs, 1400 K St., N.W., Washington, DC 20005, (202) 682-6220.

D/ART - sponsored by NIMH - find where to get help, and about the latest treatments. Request "Information About the D/ART Program." Write or call Joyce Lazar, Director, D/ART Program, National Institute of Mental Health, 5600 Fishers Lane, Room 14C-02, Rockville, MD 20857, (303) 443-4140.

DRADA - (Depressive and Related Affective Disorders Association) Johns Hopkins Hospital, 600 N. Wolfe St., Baltimore, MD 21205, (301) 955-4647.

THE NATIONAL ALLIANCE FOR THE MENTALLY ILL - for families and friends of seriously mentally ill; information, emotional support, and advocacy through local and state affiliates, 1901 Fort Myer Dr., Ste. 500, Arlington, VA 22201, (703) 524-7600.

THE NATIONAL COUNCIL OF COMMUNITY MENTAL HEALTH CENTERS - 6101 Montrose Rd., Ste. 360, Rockville, MD 20857.

THE NATIONAL DEPRESSIVE AND MANIC-DEPRESSIVE ASSOCIATION - referrals for treatment and support groups. Merchandise Mart, P.O. Box 3395, Chicago, IL 60654, (312) 939-2442.

THE NATIONAL FOUNDATION FOR DEPRESSIVE ILLNESS, INC. - referrals to support groups. P.O. Box 2257, New York, NY 10116, (212) 620-0098, 1-800-248-4344.

NIMH (National Institute of Mental Health) - Consumer Information Center, Pueblo, CO 81009. information about mental disorders and life-changing new treatments. Request, e.g.:
   "A Consumer's Guide to Mental Health Services"
   "Depression: Effective Treatments"
   "Guide to Mental Health Services"
   "Plain Talk About Depression"
   "Plain Talk About Mental Help Groups"
   "Plain Talk About the Stigma of Mental Illness"
   "You Are Not Alone"

For further information, write or call: NIMH Public Inquiries, 5600 Fishers Lane, Room 15C-05, Rockville, MD 20857, (301) 443-4513.

NATIONAL MENTAL HEALTH ASSOCIATION - referrals for treatment and support groups. 1021 Prince St., Alexandria, VA 22314-2971, (703) 684-7722.

(NOTE: Consult your phone book in case they list state and local chapters of these organizations.)

APPENDIX B

DEPRESSIVE SYMPTOMS

Persistent sad, anxious, or "empty" mood

Feelings of hopelessness, pessimism

Feelings of guilt, worthlessness, helplessness

Loss of interest or pleasure in hobbies and activities that you once enjoyed, including sex

Insomnia, early-morning awakening, or oversleeping

Appetite and/or weight loss or overeating and weight gain

Decreased energy, fatigue, being "slowed down"

Thoughts of death or suicide, suicide attempts

Restlessness, irritability

Difficulty concentrating, remembering, making decisions

Persistent physical symptoms that do not respond to treatment, such as headaches, digestive disorders, and chronic pain

MANIC SYMPTOMS

Inappropriate elation

Inappropriate irritability

Severe insomnia

Grandiose notions

Increased talking

Racing thoughts, often disconnected

Increased sexual desire

Markedly increased energy

Poor judgment, business and financial

Inappropriate social behavior

Misdirected, unwarranted anger

Anyone suffering from four or more of the above symptoms for more than two weeks, or whose usual functioning has become impaired by the symptoms, is likely to have a depressive disorder. According to NIMH, treatment is needed.

Appendix B is from D/ART pamphlet, "Depression: What you need to know," by Marilyn Sargent

APPENDIX C

HELPING THE DEPRESSED PERSON

To be the most helpful, encourage or, if necessary, insist that the depressed person get appropriate treatment. The symptoms are quite likely to stop him or her from seeking professional assistance. You could offer to make the arrangements and provide the transportation.

DO

Maintain as normal a relationship as possible.

Help the depressed person get appropriate diagnosis and treatment, as mentioned above. Be gentle, but firm.

Give the support, love, and encouragement that your relative or friend needs so desperately. Self-esteem and confidence are nonexistent in the victim of depression.

Express affection. Offer hugs when appropriate.

Encourage activity.

Compliment any efforts.

Extend reassurance and help them feel worthwhile.

Be aware of warning symptoms, (See Appendix B). Unrelieved, these and other symptoms can lead to physical problems or a suicide attempt.

Be aware of abrupt changes in mood and behavior, such as a normally gregarious person becoming silent and withdrawn.

Call Suicide Prevention or a Psychiatric Hospital for advice and help if there is talk about death or suicide or if the person starts giving away valued personal things.

DON'T

DON'T blame the person; blame the symptoms.

DON'T criticize, pick on, or show disapproval and add to the misery the person already feels.

DON'T say things like, "You just have to snap out of it," or "What's the matter with you, are you crazy?"

DON'T think you are the only one going through this bewildering experience.

DON'T think, like the person with the illness, that it is a hopeless situation.

DON'T desert him or her when you are so desperately needed.

DON'T think you have to handle this alarming problem alone.

DON'T leave a person alone if the symptoms are severe, prolonged, or there are four or more.

CHARTER HOSPITAL
OF SAN DIEGO

Mood Disorders Progam
John Feighner, MD, Director
Kent Layton, MA, Program Director
11878 Avenue of Industry
San Diego, CA 92128
1-800-622-6642

APPENDIX D

FEIGHNER-LAYTON
GLOBAL ASSESSMENT SCALE FOR MANIA
FEIGHNER
DEPRESSION SCALE

There is considerable evidence that when escalating symptoms of mood disorders are identified at an early stage, therapy and medication can reduce the symptoms of this psychobiological illncss.

If you suspect that you might have a mood disorder, evaluate the statements in the scales on the following pages.

Before you start, be aware of "medical student syndrome," "that's me syndrome," or "disease of the week club." Try to avoid the belief that normal behavior traits are the same as the disorders.

Appendix D is used by permission of the directors listed above.

FEIGHNER-LAYTON
GLOBAL ASSESSMENT SCALE FOR MANIA

Please rate how you have generally been feeling during the past week including today. Use a separate sheet of paper, so you can use the scale at different times. Indicate the date for comparison.

Key: 0=Absent 1=Mild 2=Moderate 3=Marked 4=Severe

1. Feel happy, cheerful, good   0 1 2 3 4

2. More involved than usual in social activities   0 1 2 3 4

3. More physically active than usual; at work,
   school, home   0 1 2 3 4

4. More physically restless, hard to sit still   0 1 2 3 4

5. Urge to talk in social situations   0 1 2 3 4

6. Talk faster than others   0 1 2 3 4

7. Rapid or racing thoughts   0 1 2 3 4

8. Feel especially talented   0 1 2 3 4

9. More energy than usual   0 1 2 3 4

10. More easily distracted than usual   0 1 2 3 4

11. More urge than usual to get involved in
    business or financial deals   0 1 2 3 4

12. More urge than usual to take charge in social
    situations   0 1 2 3 4

13. I dislike people who tell me what to do more than
    I usually do   0 1 2 3 4

14. Urge to comment on almost every subject of
    conversation   0 1 2 3 4

15. More likely to make "snap decisions"   0 1 2 3 4

16. Get bored easily in most conversations   0 1 2 3 4

17. Spending more money than usual   0 1 2 3 4

18. Driving faster or more dangerously than usual   0 1 2 3 4

19. Find it more stimulating to do several things
    at once   0 1 2 3 4

20. More irritable than usual   0 1 2 3 4

21. I make more late night phone calls than usual   0 1 2 3 4

22. Feeling that no matter what happens, everything
    will be all right.   0 1 2 3 4

23. Feel particularly fit and healthy   0 1 2 3 4

24. Enjoy life more than others   0 1 2 3 4

25. Feel nervous and anxious   0 1 2 3 4

26. More sexual fantasies or thoughts than usual   0 1 2 3 4

27. Decreased need for sleep   0 1 2 3 4

28. Need less than 5 hours of sleep a day   0 1 2 3 4

29. Increased religious or philosophical interests   0 1 2 3 4

30. Others question my decisions or judgments
    more than usual   0 1 2 3 4

Symptoms, to be diagnostic, have to affect in a negative manner social interaction, work, and free time. Any individual statement with a value of 3 or more may require intervention. As values of 3 or 4 increase, so does the probability of the need to seek a professional who specializes in the treatment of mood disorders. (See Appendix A for referrals and the Index under Professional help)

FEIGHNER DEPRESSION SCALE

Please rate how you have generally been feeling during the past week, including today. Use a separate sheet of paper, so you can use the scale at different times. Indicate the date for comparison.

Key: 0=Absent 1=Mild 2=Moderate 3=Marked 4=Severe

1. Depressed, sad	0 1 2 3 4
2. Good news would not cheer me up, even for a short time	0 1 2 3 4
3. Angry, irritable	0 1 2 3 4
4. Decreased self-esteem or self-confidence, low thoughts about myself	0 1 2 3 4
5. Guilt feelings, feeling like a burden to family or society	0 1 2 3 4
6. Hopelessness, things will not get better	0 1 2 3 4
7. Helplessness, I can't change things	0 1 2 3 4
8. Trouble falling asleep	0 1 2 3 4
9. Waking in the middle of the night	0 1 2 3 4
10. Waking in the morning 1-2 hours before I need to	0 1 2 3 4
11. Sleeping more than usual	0 1 2 3 4
12. Drowsy during the day	0 1 2 3 4
13. Fatigue, low energy, hard to get going	0 1 2 3 4
14. Decreased appetite	0 1 2 3 4

15. Increased appetite   0 1 2 3 4

16. Decreased weight   0 1 2 3 4

17. Increased weight   0 1 2 3 4

18. Decreased sexual interest   0 1 2 3 4

19. Increased sexual interest   0 1 2 3 4

20. Decreased interest in usual activities   0 1 2 3 4

21. Decreased involvement in usual activities-
    withdrawn   0 1 2 3 4

22. Decreased pleasure or loss of enjoyment in
    usual activities   0 1 2 3 4

23. Decreased memory   0 1 2 3 4

24. Decreased concentration   0 1 2 3 4

25. Indecisiveness-unable to make decisions   0 1 2 3 4

26. So restless I can't sit still or relax   0 1 2 3 4

27. Feeling slowed down in mind and body   0 1 2 3 4

28. Mood worse in the morning   0 1 2 3 4

29. Mood worse in the evening   0 1 2 3 4

30. Thoughts of suicide or wishing to be dead   0 1 2 3 4

31. Intent to kill self   0 1 2 3 4

32. Anxious, nervous, worried, apprehensive   0 1 2 3 4

33. Physical anxiety symptoms, like heart beating
    oddly, short of breath, tremor, sweating,   0 1 2 3 4
    butterflies in the stomach or frequent
    urination

34. So afraid of certain things or situations
    that I avoid them   0 1 2 3 4

35. Sudden, severe, unexpected feelings that
    something terrible is going to happen   0 1 2 3 4

36. Hearing voices or seeing things that are
    not there   0 1 2 3 4

37. Believing things that others do not believe   0 1 2 3 4

38. Feeling suspicious of others, that others
    want to hurt me   0 1 2 3 4

39. Unpleasant, unrealistic thoughts go over and
    over in my mind and I can't stop them   0 1 2 3 4

40. Feeling compelled to do senseless things
    over and over   0 1 2 3 4

41. Feeling I am some other person or am outside
    my body   0 1 2 3 4

42. Feeling things are not real, like in a fog or
    dream world   0 1 2 3 4

43. Worried about my physical health   0 1 2 3 4

44. Unable to control my impulses   0 1 2 3 4

Symptoms, to be diagnostic, have to affect in a negative manner social interaction, work, and free time. Any individual statement with a value of 3 or more may require intervention. As values of 3 or 4 increase, so does the probability of the need to seek a professional who specializes in the treatment of mood disorders. (See Appendix A for referrals and the Index under Professional help)

BIBLIOGRAPHY

Andersen, Samuel, T. M., M.D., "Information for Patients and Their Families About Lithium Carbonate," Long Beach, CA: printout, 1981.

"Combating the Stigma of Mental Illness," NIMH (National Institute of Mental Health), Rockville, MD: DHHS (U.S. Department of Health and Human Services) U. S. Government Printing Office, (ADM) 86-1470, Rev. 1986.

The Comprehensive Textbook of Psychiatry. Editors, Harold I. Kaplan and Benjamin J. Sadock. Fifth Edition, Baltimore, MD: Williams and Wilkins, 1989.

D/ART, (Depression/Awareness, Recognition, Treatment) NIMH, DHHS brochure reprinted, 1988.

DSMIII-R, Washington, DC: American Psychiatric Association, 1987, 213-233.

Downs, Hugh, Channel 10 at 10 p.m. "Beyond the Darkness," August 31, 1990.

Gold, Mark S., M.D. *The Good News About Depression.* New

York City: Villard Books, a division of Random House, Inc., 1987, xv, 11, 14, 55, 72, 197, 198, 246.

Guinness, Alma E., Editor. *Reader's Digest's ABC's of the Human Mind: A Family Answer Book.* Pleasantville, New York, Reader's Digest Association, 1990.

Hatfield, Agnes B. Ph.D. "The Meaning of Mental Illness to the Family," excerpted from *Coping with Mental Illness in the Family - A Family Guide,* distributed by the Alliance for the Mentally Ill of Maryland, Inc., and the Maryland Department of Health and Mental Hygiene.

"Helpful Facts About Depressive Disorders," D/ART Program, DHHS Publication, 1987, p. 5.

"Information on Lithium," NIMH, DHHS.

Jamison, Dr. Kay Redfield, Robert Winter, *Moods and Music* Concert Program, "Philosophy Underlying the Concert," San Diego, CA: C & L Printing, 1989.

Klein, Donald E., M.D., Paul H. Wender, M.D. *Do You Have a Depressive Illness?* New York: Plume Book/New American Library, 1988. ix, 1, 3, 8, 17, 55, 66.

Layton, Kent, M. A. papers that include:
"Delusions, a False Belief System of Reality."
Didactic lecture on "Bipolar Affective Disorder."
Didactic Group, "Stress and Affective Disorder," p. 1.

Leo, John, reported by William Blaylock. "The Ups and Downs of Creativity," *Time,* Oct. 8, 1984.

Lobel, Brana, and Robert M.A. Hirschfeld, M.D. "Depression, What We Know," Washington, DC: U.S. Government Printing Office, 1984.

"The Meaning of Mental Illness to the Family," a printout from Charter Hospital of San Diego.

Medical Essay: Mayo Clinic Health Letter, Rochester, MN. Mayo Foundation for Medical Education and Research, Feb. 1982.

"Mental Illness: Its Myths and Truths," booklet from National Association of Private Psychiatric Hospitals.

"Mood Disorders: Pharmacologic Prevention of Recurrences," (NIH) National Institute of Health: U.S. Government Printing Office, 1986.

Sargent, Marilyn,
    "Depression - What you Need to Know," NIMH, D/ART Program, DHHS Publication No. (ADM) 87-1543, 1987.

    "Depressive Disorders: Treatments Bring New Hope," NIMH, DHHS Pub. No. (ADM) 86-1491, 1986.

Sargent, Marilyn, Joyce Swearingen, "Depressive Disorders: Causes and Treatments," NIMH, DHHS: U.S. Government Printing Office, Reprinted 1983.

Smith, Lauren H., M.D., "When a Mental Patient Comes Home," reprint from *This Week Magazine,* copyright 1963.

"The Stigma of Mental Illness," NIMH: U.S. Government Printing Office, DHHS Publication No. (ADM) 86-1470, revised 1986.

"You Are Not Alone," NIMH, U.S. Government Printing Office, DHHS Publication (ADM) 85-1178, revised 1985.

(See Appendix A for some addresses.)

GLOSSARY

Biopsychiatrist: psychiatrist who thoroughly explores biological causes of depressive disorders when considering treatment; highly skilled in differential diagnosis and treatment

Bipolar disorder: one or more manic episodes alternating, usually, with one or more major depressive episodes. Range from mild to severe. May, or may not have psychotic features.

Bipolar disorder, mixed/intermixed: symptoms alternate, or in some cases patients experience symptoms of mania and depression at the same time.

"Blues": Not as severe, lengthy, or ongoing as major depression. Does not as seriously affect one's work, relationships, and pleasure.

Cyclothymia: mild to moderate form of bipolar disorder; may be chronic.

D/ART: (Depression/Awareness, Recognition, Treatment) national educational program on depressive disorders; for the public, primary care physicians, mental health specialists, and others who care about people. Launched by NIMH (National

Institute of Mental Health) to campaign to make depression America's newest health priority.

Depression: severe mental and emotional feelings of helplessness and hopelessness

Depressive disorder: (see Mood disorder) includes major depression and dysthymia (see Major depression and Dysthymia)

Doctor/Physician/Psychiatrist/Psychiatric Physician: terms used for psychiatric specialist and medical doctor (M.D.)

ECT/Electroconvulsive treatment: (commonly called "shock treatment" by the layman) used primarily for major depression or manic-depression. While the patient is anesthetized, current is administered for a few seconds, usually two or three times a week for four to six weeks. A small percent of patients who do not respond to medication request this treatment.

Episode: (major depressive, manic, or hypomanic) a period of time when a patient exhibits mood disorder symptoms

Euphoria: abnormal feeling of buoyant vigor and elation. Patient may be hyperactive, hostile when thwarted, grandiose, and exceedingly talkative. (See Manic)

Genetic: heredity determines inherited characteristics

High: informal word for manic euphoria

Hypomanic episode: a well-defined period of time when symptoms tend to be less severe than in manic episodes. It may or may not cause impairment, social or occupational, that requires hospitalization.

Major chronic depressive episode: current episode of two consecutive years. No period of two months or more without depressive symptoms.

Major/clinical depression: one or more major depressive episodes without any former manic or hypomanic episodes

Major melancholic episode: classic or typically severe major depressive episode. Usually worse in morning. It is believed to be responsive to medications, including lithium, certain antidepressants, and ECT. Suicidal thoughts and attempts may be a common danger.

Manic episode/phase: abnormally elevated mood. The prevailing mood can also be expansive or irritable. Symptoms cause marked problems at work, in socializing, and in relationships. May require hospitalization to avert harm to self or others.

Mixed bipolar disorder/intermixed: (See Bipolar disorder, mixed)

Mood: formerly called affect. Far-reaching, prolonged emotion or feeling, subjectively experienced and displayed mental disorders. Depression and elation, if extreme, may affect the patient's perceptions.

Mood disorder: determined by pattern of mood episodes in which symptoms meet clinical criteria. Includes bipolar and depressive disorders. Not caused by other physical or mental disorders.

Mood Syndrome: (manic or depressive) group of symptoms that meet criteria for mood disorder

Psychiatrist/physician/psychiatric physician: medical doctors (physicians) who specialize in psychiatric diagnosis and treatment. Some psychiatrists prefer to be referred to as physicians. All are qualified to prescribe medication.

Rapid Cycling: minimum of two complete cycles of manic and depressive episodes within six months

Severe/clinical/major depression: require treatment with psychotherapy, medication, or both.   Many possible causes need well-qualified diagnosis. Terms are used interchangeably.

Unipolar disorder: mood disorder of recurring depressions only

INDEX